SUDDEN POSITION GUIDE TO

Cataloging
and
Metadata

ALCTS SUDDEN POSITION SERIES #1

SUDDEN POSITION GUIDE TO
Cataloging and Metadata

Jeremy Myntti
EDITOR

SUSAN THOMAS ■ SERIES EDITOR

CONTRIBUTORS
(in alphabetical order)

BEN ABRAHAMSE
WHITNEY BUCCICONE
STEPHEN BUSS
AUTUMN FAULKNER
MATTHEW GALLAGHER
JEREMY MYNTTI
NICOLE SMELTEKOP

Association for Library Collections & Technical Services
a division of the American Library Association
CHICAGO   2019

The paper used in this publication meets the minimum requirements of American National Standard for Information Sciences—Permanence of Paper for Printed Library Materials, ANSI Z39.48-1992.

ISBNs
978-0-8389-4857-6 (print)
978-0-8389-4867-5 (PDF)

Library of Congress Cataloging-in-Publication Data
Names: Abrahamse, Ben, author. | Myntti, Jeremy, author, editor.
Title: Sudden position guide : cataloging and metadata / editor: Jeremy Myntti ; collaborators (in alphabetical order): Ben Abrahamse, Whitney Buccicone, Stephen Buss, Autumn Faulkner, Matthew Gallagher, Jeremy Myntti, Nicole Smeltekop.
Other titles: Cataloging and metadata
Description: Chicago : Collection Management Section of the Association for Library Collections & Technical Services, a division of the American Library Association, 2019. | Series: ALCTS sudden position series ; #1 | Includes bibliographical references.
Identifiers: LCCN 2019010941 (print) | LCCN 2019018017 (ebook) | ISBN 9780838948675 (ebook) | ISBN 9780838948576 (print)
Subjects: LCSH: Cataloging. | Cataloging—Standards. | Metadata. | Metadata—Standards.
Classification: LCC Z693 (ebook) | LCC Z693 .A334 2019 (print) | DDC 025.3—dc23
LC record available at https://lccn.loc.gov/2019010941

Printed in the United States of America

23 22 21 20 19   5 4 3 2 1

Contents

Foreword

The *Sudden Position* series began with an idea from Mary Miller, Director of Collection Management and Preservation at the University of Minnesota, who was serving as the chair of the ALCTS Publications Committee. She suggested creating a monographic series similar to the ALCTS Collection Management Section (CMS)'s *Sudden Selector's Guide* series, but instead of focusing on resources, it would focus on the task of positions. As our profession evolves, many of us have experienced being asked to take on additional responsibilities. I found myself in this position over twelve years ago when one year into a new position managing collection development, I was asked to take on the responsibility for acquisitions. This was a new area for me, and I looked to ALCTS to help me get up to speed. I enrolled in the Fundamentals of Acquisitions web course, which I found extremely valuable in helping me to understand and take on this new responsibility. The *Sudden Position* series, like the Fundamentals web courses, is intended to provide the reader with essential knowledge, tools of the trade, and best practices in a concise, easy to read and reference narrative format. The guides are specifically meant to help anyone who is taking on a new position or added technical services responsibility.

Susan Thomas
ALCTS Monographs Editor
March 2019

Introduction

I f you are reading this book then there is a good chance that you have some material that you want to share with people using your library, but you're not quite sure how. They might be tangibles things or digital files; they might be texts or images or recordings. Regardless of the specifics, these resources carry information that is of interest to users of your library or institution. Moreover, these resources will not stand in isolation—they will join the ranks of numerous other items in your collection. Your challenge is to ensure the objects become part of this collection without losing that which makes them distinctive and discoverable to users. And, make no mistake, it can be a challenge.

The field of cataloging and metadata management in libraries exists because every library, museum, archive, or other information-centered institution shares this problem: they have numerous resources and discriminating users who rely on them to help find the specific items they seek. The problem is perennial; with each passing year, more resources are created, acquired, or licensed by libraries, then made discoverable so people can locate and access them. This book aims to show you both the time-honored and emerging approaches to this problem that are practiced in the field.

Given that the word "sudden" appears prominently in the title of this book, there is also a high probability that you come to this problem feeling somewhat unprepared, perhaps even hesitant about facing it. If this is the case, please take a moment, breathe deeply, and say to yourself, "Don't panic."

While it is true that this work has its challenges, they are by no means insurmountable. While cataloging and metadata are technical disciplines and have developed their own practices and vocabularies that can be quite specific, the logical framework underneath is neither unduly complicated nor nearly as obscure as it may at first appear. We will show you throughout this monograph that the "mysterious" art of cataloging is really a form of common sense systematically applied to a set of problems librarians have grappled with for centuries.

Another reason to curb your panic is that there is no such thing as "perfect" in the world of cataloging and metadata. The possibilities of what one can say about any resource are virtually infinite, but the resources at our disposal are typically constrained by the real world. Catalogers and metadata librarians are forever making choices about where to devote resources, and in particular, their most precious resource—their time. Your time is equally precious and because of that, one of the objects of this book is an efficient introduction to rules, instructions, policies, and best practices.

If you are still feeling anxious, know that you are not in this by yourself. Cataloging and metadata are inherently social and collective endeavors. Modern cataloging and metadata management is built on the assumption that the information we collect about the objects in our collections is meant to be shared, not just with our users, but with colleagues across the country, and the world. Catalogers and metadata providers are great believers in reusing existing metadata whenever possible and in sharing metadata in ways that enable other communities to add their own expertise. Ideally, cataloging and metadata creates and sustains a virtuous cycle among users and creators of information resources, for the mutual benefit of all. The authors of this book hope to provide you with the tools and know-how to participate responsibly in the sharing economy that exists among cataloging and metadata-creating individuals and organizations.

This book is designed not only to help you with the immediate problems and tasks that are on your desk right now, but also provide you with a deeper understanding of why catalogers and metadata professionals continue to work in this stimulating field and enjoy talking and writing about it every chance they get. There is insufficient room in this monograph to give you an in-depth knowledge of each tool or resource. Instead, our goal is to give you a solid grasp of the principles of resource description, outline the practical skills you need for your specific position, familiarize you with the tools you will use on a daily basis, and help you focus your learning so you can get a running start.

The collection discovery environment is composed of five interlocking parts that work together to get information into the hands of users: the resources themselves, the metadata describing those resources, the Cataloging and Metadata Librarian (CML), the user's needs, and the discovery systems. As you move forward in this book, keep these components in mind as a framework for the specific tools, resources, and practices we discuss.

Chapter 1, "So You're Suddenly a Cataloger," takes a high-level look at what it means to be a (CML), with a focus on understanding the needs of library users in order to ensure the discoverability of resources. Chapter 2, "The Theoretical Principles of Resource Description," provides an overview of the different frameworks, content standards, and encoding standards used by CMLs, as well as the ideas and goals behind them. This will lay down the foundation you need for your new responsibilities—both the logistical and philosophical considerations that shape descriptive work.

In Chapter 3, "Learning the Standards: Cataloging," you will find a practical breakdown of the different standards related to traditional library cataloging such as Machine-Readable Cataloging (MARC), Resource Description and Access (RDA), International Standard Bibliographic Description (ISBD), controlled vocabularies, classification systems, and more. Chapter 4, "Learning the Standards: Metadata," discusses non-MARC resource descriptions, including descriptive, structural, administrative, and technical metadata. Both of these chapters will get you started on the nitty gritty skills you'll need for daily work.

Chapter 5, "Things You Might Encounter," covers many different material types that you might encounter while describing resources. Helpful tips are included with each material type to show the unique descriptive elements and special considerations that must be addressed. Chapter 6, "Tools of the Trade," is an easy reference guide to the array of standards, guidelines, best practices, professional organizations, and continuing education channels that inform and support descriptive work, along with additional resources to learn more about each one. Again, these chapters will be useful for tackling the day-to-day work crossing your desk.

The final chapter will help you look forward. It explores possible future environments for cataloging and metadata work in light of its continually evolving standards. It also offers advice for advocating for your new work at your own institution and preparing for inevitable change.

It is our hope that this concise overview of the cataloging and metadata landscape will offer you a quick but high-quality jumpstart in your new professional endeavor. Descriptive work is an essential and long-standing component of maintaining any cultural heritage collection and making it accessible to end users. You are now a part of this complicated but rewarding cultural endeavor. Welcome to the field!

Chapter ONE

So You're Suddenly a Cataloger

You may have heard the words "cataloging" and "metadata" used, more or less interchangeably, to describe activities associated with enabling resource discovery in libraries and other information-centered institutions. There is a great deal of overlap between the two, so much so that in some contexts they are used as virtual synonyms. Yet there are subtle, but important differences between the two terms which are worth considering.

Presumably, everyone knows what a catalog is: a detailed, ordered account of a collection of things. You may think of toy or other manufacturer's catalogs, gallery catalogs, or even university course catalogs. These catalogs play different roles in society but share common features: they provide enough relevant descriptive information about each item in the catalog for a user to build a picture of it in their mind. They also provide a name and/or code that the reader can use to refer to the item quickly and unambiguously. When an item is available in various, slightly different iterations, the catalog provides enough information for its readers to select the specific one they want. Each catalog is laid out and designed in such a way as to make it easy to browse and typically contains an index that facilitates quick lookups of particular items by name or other feature. Finally, they provide a system (an order form, for example) that allows users to access their selected items.

Libraries and other cultural heritage institutions likewise have catalogs, which fulfill the same functions. Be it an old-fashioned card catalog, or a state-of-the-art, web-scale discovery portal, a library's catalog is an all-important gateway that connects library patrons to the various information-carrying objects—or "resources"—in its collections. It enables patrons to find what they are looking for because the catalog provides correct and useful information about each item in the collection. Catalogs also provide ways for users who have less-specific questions about the collection to browse through and see what the library has to offer according to various topics or groupings. Finally, like the catalogs discussed above, a library's catalog is connected to other library systems, such as the stacks and circulation desk, that enable a user to get their hands on whatever resources they've selected.

In many libraries and knowledge institutions, the term "cataloging" refers to the work of keeping the library's catalog up-to-date and making sure that it continues to serve the evolving needs of the library's patrons. Administratively, it is most often associated with technical services: the area of library work that is "concerned with the acquisition, organization (bibliographic control), physical processing, and maintenance of library collections." As this definition suggests, catalogers' chief role resides in providing organization over the library's collections, as well as making it possible for the library to assert a degree of "bibliographic control" over how those resources are to be discovered and obtained or accessed. That means that catalogers work to create and maintain organizing structures such as indexes, shelf-lists or inventory, and authority files, which enable library users to understand and interact with library materials as an organic and navigable collection of resources, rather than just a jumble of documents.

To perform this task, catalogers work with metadata. Unlike "catalog," use of the word "metadata" is not as longstanding—in fact it really comes out of the last quarter of the twentieth century and reflects the growing role of computers and digital automation in library work and cataloging in particular. Let's unpack this important, though often misunderstood, term.

A well-worn cliché is that metadata is "data about data." While not incorrect, it is perhaps not particularly helpful in achieving a working understanding of what the term means. More important is what metadata *does.* The reason to record "data about data" is to provide a needed context to that data.

To help understand this, imagine a conference room full of people. They are gathered for a meeting of some kind, and perhaps some of them know each other, but perhaps not. A good step on the part of the meeting organizers would be to provide the people attending the meeting with blank name tags and a few Sharpies so the attendees can identify themselves on their lapels. Thus identified, the attendees of the meeting can proceed without the formalities of making introductions, or worse, the embarrassment of reintroductions.

You might see how this analogy begins to apply to metadata: labeling information objects is, of course, a good first step toward useful metadata. But it is not quite yet "metadata" in the complete sense. Giving meeting attendees blank placards with which to identify themselves is useful, but it could still give rise to misunderstandings. What should people write down? Their first name only, their whole name, their name and affiliation? If someone writes on their name tag the word "RAND" does that mean his name is Rand? Or that he works for the RAND Corporation? With foresight, a more fastidious meeting organizer might address this problem by handing out tags that are not completely blank, but instead are printed with the words "HELLO, MY NAME IS." This would encourage meeting attendees to provide information that the meeting organizer considers useful: whatever name they would use when introducing themselves.

Now, a "HELLO, MY NAME IS" name tag might not look much like elements that CMLs work with, but, by adding "data about data" to a tag, the meaning of the information that gets filled in on the tag is placed in a more precise semantic context. This is crucial as it enables the information to be used in other applications. It is not just data but *meta*data. We will revisit some of the mechanics of how metadata functions, is created, and maintained in further chapters.

Cataloging and metadata are related concepts. Cataloging is a service performed on behalf of the library and its users—the ongoing management of the discoverability of the library's collections. Metadata is a product that is created or curated as the essential means by which that service is carried out. When metadata librarians edit or enhance records, they are performing a cataloging function. When catalogers describe new acquisitions, they are contributing metadata to the world. Because the two concepts are tightly interwoven, the way they are used in libraries is often inconsistent. An example of this is in job titles and descriptions. Recently, there is a detectable movement away from the term "cataloger" in favor of titles that include the word "metadata," such as "Metadata Librarian" or "Metadata Manager." Another general distinction might be that catalogers more often engage directly in the *production* of metadata and metadata librarians in the *management* (transformation, enhancement, etc.) of metadata. These are generalizations, and professionals in these fields rely on essentially the same set of skills and knowledge regardless of title. For consistency's sake, in this book we will use the term "Cataloging / Metadata Librarian" (CML) when discussing individuals working in this field. Also, see the beginning of Chapter 4 for additional discussion about the distinctions between cataloging and metadata work.

FRONT OF THE HOUSE
Understanding User Needs

Ultimately, cataloging and metadata management are about communication. CMLs work to communicate information about a re-source—what it is and what it's about, where it came from and what it's for—to an audience of users. However, unlike many forms of communication with which we are familiar, the metadata CMLs create is typically not read directly by the user, but mediated by a system (the catalog or discovery portal). This means that some of the metadata CMLs manage is related to fulfilling systems-needs, and some is more directed as users themselves. Throughout this book you may notice that, frequently, CMLs record essentially the same type of information (for example, the name of an author) in two different ways: as it appears in the resource, and as it should appear for the system to index it.

Another way discovery metadata differs from typical forms of communication has to do with the underlying purpose of the messages we are sending. Our metadata does not deliver news or tell stories, but rather acts as a stand-in, or "surrogate" for a resource that exists in a library's collections. Users will probably not interact with or read all of the information a library system presents to them about a given resource, only enough to determine whether they want it. We must never forget this important aspect of metadata management as a communicative act: the value of a particular record lies primarily in how quickly and effortlessly a user can under- stand, judge, and act on what the record represents, not in the metadata itself.

Because of this, we need to get to know our users and their general and specifics needs.

Primary User Tasks

Users commonly approach the library's discovery interface with one of two problems. The first is when users are trying to find a particular resource in the library. We call this a "known item search." While this appears to be a simple task, it can be complex depending on what information the user is able to provide. If a user has complete bibliographic information—say a citation from an article or a bibliography—then that is a straightforward matter to resolve. Often, however, users do not have complete (or accurate) knowledge of a resource's bibliographic particulars. Therefore catalogs, and the metadata that support them, must be able to provide users with the ability to search or browse according to various bibliographic criteria—pieces of information that describe a resource, such as the name of the author, the place and date of publication, the publisher name, and more.

"Known item" searches illustrate a basic function of the catalog and its metadata: when provided with a set of information (a "query"), the catalog should be able to retrieve a representation of every resource that matches. Suppose a user wants *The Little Prince* by Antoine de Saint-Exupéry. They provide the catalog with the information they know: "title = Little Prince." The result of this basic search will be one of three possibilities: there is nothing in the collection with that title, the one resource in the collection with the title Little Prince, or a set of multiple results, which the user must inspect to find the book in question. Based on the results returned, the user may decide to abandon the search, modify the search, or act on the search.

A second common user task is to find resources about a particular subject or in a certain genre. This is often called a "topical" or "subject search" where a user wants to discover the resources a library has on a particular topic. To fulfill these requests the catalog must contain metadata, not only about where an item comes from (bibliographic metadata), but also regarding what the item is about ("subject metadata"). Of course, in most instances, the subject(s) of a particular resource are not fully evident from that resource's title, so catalogers must provide additional information—"subject headings" or "subject keywords"—that reflect the topical content of the resources.

This basic type of user problem illustrates another primary function of the catalog. When a user wants a specific item, searching the catalog is the most effective means of finding it. But when the user's goal is to discover and access something not specific but rather a range of resources on a topic, they want to be able to shop before they order. Thus catalogs must also provide the ability to browse a library's collections in various ways. For example, suppose our user who was looking for *The Little Prince* is intrigued by the fact that its author was a famous pilot. They might want to see what resources the library has on aviators and browsing the catalog by the relevant subject term is an effective way to solve this problem. They then can see a sorted list of relevant results and pick the ones of interest.

"Searching" and "browsing" comprise the two basic user functions of the catalog. The search function enables users to retrieve specific results by providing bits of known information. The browse function, by contrast, allows users to inspect a sorted set of results and pick the ones that seem most relevant. Of course, not all "known item" problems are resolved through searching, and not every "subject" question is resolved by browsing. While we have presented these as two distinct functions for the purpose of discussion, most real-life user tasks involve a fair amount of switching back-and-forth between the two. A user may search on a term, then browse through the results; likewise, a user might browse an index to find useful search terms. What is important to recognize is that the catalog, and the metadata it runs on, must support both of user interaction.

More Complex User Needs

Indexes

Some users may need to browse the catalog in a more intensive way. For example, instead of just finding all resources under a particular topic, a user may want to browse the various topics under which resources are organized in a catalog. Or a user may wish to view a list of authors and other individuals who are related to resources in the collections. Catalogs typically provide users with the ability to browse various indexes, which are alphabetically sorted lists of terms that provide reference to records in the catalog.

Different systems will provide different indexes for users to browse, but the most common are an index of names (individuals and organizations) related to resources in the collection and an index of subject terms—words or phrases that have been supplied to describe what the resources in a collection are about. Many catalogs provide a "name-title" index which is an index of all resources in a library's collections organized alphabetically by the name of the author(s) or by the title of the resource. That is to say that resources with identifiable authors are indexed under the name of the author while resources that, for various reasons (some of which we will look at later) do not have single, identifiable authors, are placed in the same alphabetical order according to their titles. Finally, catalogs typically provide a "shelf list," an index of all resources in the catalog sorted by their call number or acquisition number. This serves primarily as an inventory control mechanism for librarians who maintain the catalog, though users may also use it to perform a "virtual browse" of the shelves.

The key features of catalog indexes, besides the fact that they are sorted alphabetically, are as follows. First, the individual entries in a catalog index are managed by librarians according to library principles. For example, an overriding principle of indexing names of individuals is that, outside of a few exceptional circumstances, each individual who is related to a resource in the library's collections appears in only one place in the index. Authors whose names change, or more commonly, do not change but appear in slightly different formats on different resources (John Smith vs. Jonathan Smith, for example) are provided with a single entry (or "heading") in the catalog. Thus catalogers might bring together into the index different representations of an individual, which might otherwise remain distinct and possibly be construed to the user as two different people. Bringing together under a single heading or entry various resources that would otherwise be separate is called "collocation." The inverse of collocation is equally important when, as frequently happens, two completely separate individuals happen to share the same name. CMLs must ensure that they are represented separately and not allow the resources with which they are connected to become commingled in the index. To do this, they provide additional distinguishing information to one or the other heading; this process is called "disambiguation" because it is a proactive attempt to avoid potential ambiguity between two identically named individuals.

Finally, catalog indexes employ "cross referencing" to assist users in arriving at the correct entry or heading in the index. We have already mentioned the example of an individual whose name appears one way on a particular resource and another way on others. The CML will intervene to ensure that all the resources appear, in the index, under one form of the name. But what about the other form? Depending on how different that alternate form of name is, the user may or may not see, when they browse the index, that resources have been "relocated" to a different spot in the index. So a common and important practice in managing indexes is to provide a "*see*" reference at one entry to point the user toward the "correct" entry. As one might imagine this see reference instructs the user "For resources by/related to this individual, see the index under this other form of their name." The see reference is an important form of cross referencing, perhaps the most important, but there are others. Sometimes the relationship between two entities in the catalog is not one of replacement (use this for that) but rather of supplement. A user will find resources related to an individual in the index at a certain point, but also under a different, related entry. For this there is the "*see also*" reference. This is an instruction not to "relocate" to a different place, but rather to continue looking in another specified place in the index for additional relevant resources.

As you might have figured out, the overriding goal of managing library indexes—collocating, disambiguating, and providing cross-referencing—is to ensure that, for each logical entity in the catalog (each author, resource, and subject area) there is a single place where all relevant resources can be found. A catalog index is, at least in theory, exhaustive; it shows every resource in the collection created by a particular author or on a particular topic. This is an extremely challenging objective because library collections, like libraries themselves, are living, growing organisms. Technological changes have driven much of this growth in the direction of digital acquisition, which raises particular challenges to the goal of maintaining a catalog's indexes and the metadata that underlie them. As library catalogs increasingly move out of "silos" (the individual, bespoke systems they have traditionally run on) and into more universal discovery applications, this challenge is bound to become even harder to surmount. Nonetheless the principle of a unified, exhaustive, and useful index to the entirety of a library's collections remains important.

Facets and Filters in the Catalog

In addition to the basic keyword or title/author search discussed above, there are usually options to further narrow the results displayed to a user by a library system. *Facets* are options that can be activated to allow users to filter results based on language, genre, format, year published, and more. This allows the user to control the result list based on their own personal need and winnow out results that may be less relevant to their query. An institution can generally turn these options on and off as needed within their own catalog/discovery system.

BEHIND THE SCENES
Objectives of a Cataloging or
Metadata System

In the preceding section we've outlined the primary ways in which users interact with library systems to discover resources that are relevant to their needs. The discussion has been limited to users' points-of-view because it is ultimately by fulfilling users' needs that catalogs, and the CMLs who manage them, succeed or fail.

Now we turn to considering how the situation looks from the other side of the catalog, where you, the CML, find yourself. As we have seen, users use catalogs to answer questions (search) and to examine (browse) and refine (facets/filtering) results about a library's collected resources. They also typically begin their interaction with the catalog by providing some bit of information of their own (a criterion) that will drive the search process. The overriding question for catalogers and metadata librarians is what type of criteria are users likely to provide, and how can we ensure that users receive accurate results to their queries.

Catalogers and metadata librarians are, and have always been, keen to find answers to these questions and have generally proceeded in a collaborative fashion by developing shared principles and standards for describing resources and providing access to them (managing the way elements in the description are presented in indexes, etc.). Much of what we will talk about in the remainder of this book is built on this shared understanding of how our metadata should serve user needs, from models and descriptive standards down to practical guidelines for specific types of material. And all of these models and practices are built on this foundation of a shared understanding of what it is users want or need from the cataloger.

The idea of a set of user-focused principles that would guide the creation and management of a catalog is part of the rich heritage of cataloging theory and practice. The classic statement of what users should expect from a catalog appeared in the preface to Charles Ammi Cutter's *Rules for a Dictionary Catalog* (1876; 4th rev. ed., 1904) as a list of "Objects" and "Means" of his dictionary catalog. The three objects Cutter identifies are "to enable a person to find a book," "to show what the library has," and "to assist in the choice of a book." In many ways what is remarkable about this statement, first published in the late nineteenth century, is that it predates much of the technological infrastructure that CMLs now use, yet the "objects" (and to a lesser degree "the means") Cutter presents still resonate.

In 1961, the International Federation of Library Associations (IFLA) hosted an international conference in Paris, France, the goal of which was to develop agreed upon principles for what catalogs and metadata (though the term did not exist at the time) should do. This conference released an important set of principles that are often referred to as the "Paris principles." The second of these stated principles asserts, "The catalogue should be an efficient instrument for ascertaining whether the library contains a particular book . . .

OBJECTS. *

1. To enable a person to find a book of which either
    (A) the author
    (B) the title   } is known.
    (C) the subject
2. To show what the library has
    (D) by a given author
    (E) on a given subject
    (F) in a given kind of literature.
3. To assist in the choice of a book
    (G) as to its edition (bibliographically).
    · (H) as to its character (literary or topical).

MEANS.

1. Author-entry with the necessary references (for A and D).
2. Title-entry or title-reference (for B).
3. Subject-entry, cross-references, and classed subject-table (for C and E).
4. Form-entry and language-entry (for F).
5. Giving edition and imprint, with notes when necessary (for G).
6. Notes (for H).

FIGURE 1

Charles A. Cutter (1837–1903), an American pioneer of cataloging and author of the celebrated Rules for a Dictionary Catalog. He is eponymous for the term "to cutter," used by catalogers as a shorthand for assigning an alphanumeric "author" or "work number," a practice he advocated for in his work and writing.[2]

[and] which works by a particular author and which editions of a particular work are in the library." What is noteworthy about this statement, when compared with Cutter's, is the focus on the catalog as an inventory-management system (albeit, a user-focused one). By 1961, Cutter's Alphabetical catalog had become an "efficient instrument" for users to determine, primarily, whether the collection has what they want. The final clause, "which edition of a particular work," reflects a greater concern with the precise identification of editions of works—resources that are published and collected in multiple forms. What the 1961 Paris Principles look toward is the idea that an essential function of the catalog is to provide identification of information resources, so that users can determine with precision that the resource as presented by the catalog matches what they are looking for. Ultimately this question of identifying editions of a particular work would become a central preoccupation of many cataloging theorists.

In the late 1990s, another seminal document was released by IFLA. This was the result of a study group that IFLA had sponsored to think about international principles for describing information resources. The result of this group was an influential report, *Functional Requirements for Bibliographic Records* (1998, rev. 2008). The ambitious effort sought to establish "a framework that identifies and clearly defines the entities of interest to users of bibliographic records" and "a conceptual model" that would help determine what descriptive elements relate to "the various tasks that users perform when consulting bibliographic records." In other words, what is often referred to as "the FRBR report" sought to answer the same question Cutter and others have asked: what type of information should we collect on behalf of users, and what can users expect to be able to do with this information? The report approached this question by defining what it calls "generic tasks that are performed by users." The four tasks that are identified are:

Find: Using the information within records to find those records that match a user's stated needs. Unlike previous statements we've looked at, the FRBR report does not provide a closed list of attributes a user can expect to FIND records on, but provides familiar examples (a subject search, or a title search).

Identify: Being able to confirm (or disprove), through a sufficiency of informative details in the record, that the particular resource a user is seeking is represented by that record. In other words, the IDENTIFY function is about the metadata in a record being precise enough that users can tell if it's "the one" they're looking for.

Select: Like Cutter's hope that the catalog will "assist in the choice of a book as to its edition . . . and its character," the SELECT user task is about enabling users to pick, among various similar resources in the collection, those that are appropriate to their needs. This could be, for example, enabling users to select the version of a novel that is in their preferred language or having users choose whether they want to check out a print book or read the electronic version.

Obtain: To the three familiar user tasks above, the FRBR report adds, ". . . using the data in order to acquire or obtain access to the entity described." Some of the metadata in a catalog must be devoted to informing users how to get their hands on (or point their browsers at) the content they are looking for. This might be things like location information and call numbers for print books or the URL of a web resource. This user task recognizes that the library catalog is embedded in the collections and services of the larger library and helps to close the final distance between library users and the resources they are looking for.

The 1998 FRBR report outlined only four user tasks. A recently issued document, *IFLA Library Reference Model: A Conceptual Model for Bibliographic Information* (2017), identifies the same four user tasks of the FRBR Report and adds a fifth to the list:

Explore: "To discover resources using the relationships between them." In other words, browsing the catalog or some other system, moving from one entry to another by following the links (either bibliographic or topical) that connect them, is recognized as an essential user task.

It is difficult to overstate the importance of these "objectives" to CMLs. They act as a set of boundaries, which serve to keep catalogers from creating too much metadata. These five "user tasks" or "catalog objectives" provide catalogers with a set of parameters against which to assess the value of the metadata they create and manage. The underlying principle is that metadata must be able to serve at least one of these fundamental objectives, otherwise its value as bibliographic metadata is questionable.

These objectives also provide CMLs with a framework (or "conceptual model," as the FRBR report calls it) by which to understand, in broad terms, how catalogs function as intermediaries between librarians and users. We can use these five "generic user tasks" to test whether changes to a system or index are valuable. These principles can drive developers of catalog systems to create new ways for users to interact with the metadata or drive librarians to advocate to their vendors for such changes.

From the point-of-view of a practicing librarian, these five object-ives, taken together, are extremely ambitious in scope. We know that our systems and the metadata they contain are not always sufficient or precise enough to enable users to find, identify, select, obtain, and navigate among the resources in our collections as they are represented in the catalog. Reality is always less than perfect, but this ambition is salutary, inasmuch as it keeps CMLs focused on the fact that the value of their work stems ultimately from how it helps users, even though they may never meet them face to face.

WHERE DISCOVERY AND DESCRIPTION HAPPENS

As mentioned above, we've decided to use the catch-all term "catalog" in this book to denote the place where users search any given collection based on the descriptive metadata of its resources. Within the cataloging and metadata communities, however, there are more specific terms in place that we use to further delineate what type of catalog we're talking about and what type of counterpart systems we work with to input metadata and manage collections.

While the principles of resource description based on user be-havior described above and outlined more extensively in Chapter 2 are paramount, it is also important to consider the nature of the public-facing catalog you are using and the backend system that manages your metadata. Each system has its own purposes, capa-cities, and limitations, among other considerations, that will likely affect the way in which you approach your cataloging and metadata description practices.

Below is a concise summary of the big picture things to keep in mind when considering where discovery and description cur-rently happens at your institution. The way in which these com-ponents interact with each other make up the fundamental digital infrastructure where the work of most CMLs takes place.

Integrated Library Systems (ILSs) vs. Library Services Platforms (LSPs)

To start, when the cataloging and metadata community refers to cataloging, it is typically referring to MARC21-based description that is inputted and managed in ILSs and LSPs. Speaking in generalities, ILSs and LSPs tend to manage bibliographic data of a collection's circulating and non-circulating print and electronic resources, so they can be searched and retrieved via the catalog they are connected to. ILSs are searchable via Online Public Access Catalogs (OPACs) whereas LSPs are typically integrated into Discovery Layers, which is further elaborated upon below. Neither ILSs nor LSPs typically store digital representations of those resources, such as text, audio, and video files, although this feature will likely be integrated into LSPs over time. Many CML's work within these systems as part of their daily responsibilities.

Currently, we are in the midst of a massive shift in technology as libraries migrate away from their ILSs towards LSPs. To provide some brief context, ILSs were initially developed in the mid-to-late 1990s to manage predominantly print collections. To date, they have valuably served their original purpose for collections of varying sizes and scopes. Some examples include Innovative's Millennium, Ex Libris' Voyager, and SirsiDynix's Symphony. Certain libraries are reluctant to shift to new systems for a myriad of reasons such as staffing concerns, budget shortfalls, data security issues, etc. However, both vendors and other libraries have noticed the age of these legacy systems and developed more contemporary systems that are, in general, more user friendly and more efficient at managing the entirety of a library's print and electronic collection. Further, many ILSs are hosted on local servers and require routine maintenance by internal staff members.

The LSPs that have been developed over the last five or so years are most often web-based, exhibit a greater degree of interoperability with other pertinent systems, offer more advanced and streamlined reporting functionality, and are better equipped at managing electronic resources. Since the marketplace is quite competitive at the moment and LSPs often consolidate multiple pre-existing services, migrating to LSPs can represent a cost savings or remain cost neutral for libraries over the life of a new contract. Some examples of contemporary LSPs are Ex Libris's Alma, OCLC's WMS, SirsiDynix's BLUEcloud, Innovative's Sierra, Innovative's Polaris, and FOLIO (still in development as of this publication).

There are a number of ramifications for the sudden CML implicit in this systems shift. Most importantly, technical services librarians often play key roles during the selection of an LSP and in the subsequent migration process. They are relied upon to ask pertinent questions regarding the functionality of common cataloging workflows within the current ILS and the LSPs being considered. After a selection is made, they also have to provide key information to the vendor in question about the overall bibliographic nature of the collection, including identifying any local record sets that may not conform to recognized standards. They also must check the integrity of that pre-existing bibliographic data after it is loaded into the new LSP to ensure no mapping errors corrupted specific fields or record sets. It is important to keep these things in mind when thinking about the system you're currently working with and being aware of if your administration is considering a migration of some sort.

Marshall Breeding's annual Library Systems report is a very informative reference point into which types of libraries (academic, public, special, etc.) are using which management systems, including how many have migrated away from their old systems.[3]

OPACs vs. Discovery Layers

Since OPACs are tied to ILSs, they are also being rapidly replaced or supplemented by discovery layers in one form or another. OPACs, also referred to as the classic library catalog, typically allow the user to search only bibliographic records maintained in the ILS. For many of the same reasons given above, plus the added consideration of user familiarity and advanced search configurability, some libraries continue to use their OPACs and are reluctant to phase them out. On the other hand, both vendors and libraries have noticed the age of classic OPACs from both a user experience perspective and a lack of functionality for discovering electronic resources that are not described within the ILS, such as articles or resources found in digital repositories.

In contrast to OPACs, discovery layers offer more robust mechanisms to search the entirety of a library's collection. First, many have a centralized index of article-level content so that the user's research experience is more akin to searching other databases, like those offered by Google Scholar, EBSCO, ProQuest, Worldcat, PubMed, etc. Second, the user experience offered by discovery layers is being informed by extensive usability studies geared to account for a broad spectrum of basic and advanced use. Further, they typically can be configured in a number of ways to enhance their usability for the specific communities they serve. The majority of discovery layers also include the ability to harvest bibliographic records using the Open Archives Initiative Protocol for Metadata Harvesting (OAI-PMH). This capacity allows a discovery layer to collect metadata from other sources, like digital repositories, in an attempt to unify any number of cultural heritage collections into a single unified search portal and user experience. Some examples of discovery layers are Ex Libris's Primo, ProQuest's Summon, EBSCO's EDS, OCLC's Worldshare, Villanova's VuFind, and open-source Blacklight.

Again, there are ramifications any sudden CML should consider depending on how users are searching for bibliographic data in their given system. One of the most important decisions you will likely have to make is determining how much time to spend on cataloging bibliographic records and at what level of detail. You should carefully consider what is displaying in the brief and full records, what fields are included in a keyword search, and so on. You should also try to get usage statistics to see how people are searching and what they are clicking on, if that type of data is available to you. For example, if no one is clicking on specific facets, perhaps they are less important to your community and you can spend less time worrying about them. Or, if you are aware that the table of contents field isn't included in a basic keyword search in your system, then perhaps that field merits less attention than other more important fields such as title, authorized author, publication date, etc.

Digital Repositories

Digital repositories are collections of resources, typically institutional or disciplinary in nature, that have either been digitized in some form or were born so. Many libraries, archives, and museums maintain some form of digital repository in order to disseminate their special collections, institutional research output, ephemera, and other resources in a more curated and visual fashion than OPACs and discovery layers allow for. Also, a library's digital repository is primarily populated with resources with the correct copyright clearance to distribute openly or as part of the public domain.

Like the various solutions available to manage regular library collections and the considerations they merit, digital repositories offer many similar parallels. However, as digital repositories emerged later than the first-generation ILSs and must account for a wider range of metadata schemas beyond MARC, the digital repository landscape and marketplace can be a bit more complex than for library management systems. Furthermore, since digital repositories trend towards making information freely available to the public, there has been a lot more open access development and homegrown spinoffs comparatively, which will be further discussed below. Since the front-end "catalog" is often uniquely branded for the respective institution, the term "digital repository" generally encompasses both the front-end catalog (or portal) for users and the back-end interface where CMLs input metadata.

Proprietary vs. Open Source Solutions

For each class of system described above, there are both open-source and proprietary solutions available. There are a few important distinctions between the two and some considerations to make that often depend on the size and scope of your institution and collections, the skill sets of the workforce, and leadership's vision. From a systems thinking perspective, try to conceptualize how the dynamic below is approached at your own institution, as it will likely play some role in your job.

To start, there may be a strong preference regarding whether the out-of-the-box functionality and customer support offered by a commercial vendor's systems is more desirable compared to the greater interoperability, control, and customization that is often afforded by open source solutions. For example, a small library staff with limited technical skills may be more likely to choose a commercial vendor's solution since the subscription cost for a proprietary system pales in comparison to hiring additional technical staff and building out an IT infrastructure to support an open access system. Conversely, a very large institution with diverse collections and a robust IT department might find the advantages of administering an open access system to be greater than paying vendors a relatively large annual sum for a product that they have limited ability to customize.

In addition, there is a strong ethical component to supporting open access initiatives across the cultural heritage communities that cannot be overstated. Since we are tasked with preserving information and promoting accessibility, many believe that continual support for open access initiatives will reduce access barriers for everyone. From making research and educational materials available to less developed countries to protecting the public domain, many view the development and maintenance of open access systems as vitally important to their professional mission statement. This support typically manifests itself by redirecting spending away from proprietary solutions and hiring developers and project managers to collaborate on open access initiatives with peers at like-minded institutions.

To make matters slightly more convoluted, some vendors and consortia have adopted open access systems and offer hosted solutions to them with varying levels of support. This type of hybrid service serves as an interim solution between the two options discussed above and helps lesser equipped libraries support open access systems. A few examples include ByWater Solutions providing support and hosting for Koha open source ILS as well as the Lyrasis consortium hosting an Islandora open access repository solution. While ByWater and Lyrasis are still subject to the development and roadmap schedules set out by the open access communities responsible for Koha and Islandora, respectively, they are able to offer vendor-like support at substantially less cost than a vendor who needed to invest in the research and development of a standalone proprietary system.

Hosted Solutions vs. Local Installations

Similar to the proprietary versus open source debate, the decision between hosted solutions versus local installations of any component of your collection management and discovery infrastructure is largely influenced by cost; size and scope of your community and collections; staff skills; and leadership vision. Data security is also a major concern depending on the nature of patron data within these systems as well as whether the systems are connected to other vital components of your institution's larger IT infrastructure.

In short, a hosted solution means that someone outside of your institution is maintaining the IT infrastructure that allows a system to function; whereas, hosting the system locally means it is installed on local infrastructure and maintained within your institution.

Maintaining and monitoring network structure and performance as well as installing software and subsequent updates or versions is not likely going to be asked of a CML, yet we are often the first to notice performance issues or the availability of new releases. As such, it is important to know where to route requests of this nature and to understand the fundamental structure of the system you are using.

One important distinction to keep in mind is the rollout of releases in cloud-hosted environments. Since newer library systems are built around cloud computing infrastructure, new releases are generally implemented by vendors across the entire platform on a rigid schedule without the option for customers to retain a previous version or delay implementation. The result of this is a more dynamic product that is continually tweaked to enhance performance for all customers, but the lack of control over product changes is a cause of frustration for some users.

NOTES

1. Reitz, Joan M., ODLIS: online dictionary of information science. 1994. www.abc-clio.com/ODLIS/odlis_about.aspx.

2. Portrait (public domain), accessed January 4, 2019, https://en.wikipedia .org/wiki/Charles_Ammi_Cutter#/media/File:CharlesAmmiCutter_Boston Athenaeum.png. Page image (public domain): Charles A. Cutter, Rules for a printed dictionary catalogue. (Washington, D.C.: U.S. G.P.O., 1875): p. 10. https://catalog.hathitrust.org/Record/009394960.

3. Breeding, Marshall. Library Systems Report 2017. https://american libraries magazine.org/2017/05/01/library-systems-report-2017.

CHAPTER TWO

Theoretical Principles of Resource Description

As outlined in the previous chapter, the role of CMLs is to describe materials in order to enable users to find, identify, select, obtain, and explore resources. The descriptive process centers on a few basic tasks: (1) recording the identifying attributes of a resource (i.e. "describing" the resource); (2) recording the identity and role of people and groups associated with the resource being described; (3) recording significant relationships between the resource being described and other resources. As an example, suppose you are tasked with recording metadata about a *Pride & Prejudice* graphic novel. You would want to convey to a user that: (1) this is a primarily visual printed work of fiction, illustrated in color and published in 2010; (2) British nineteenth-century author Jane Austen is responsible for the basic content, but story adapter Nancy Butler and artist Hugo Petrus also share some responsibility; and (3) this is an adaptation of the original text of *Pride & Prejudice,* published in 1813.

Anything in the vast corpus of content created or curated by humans throughout history—the "universe of discourse" as the Library Reference Model (LRM) puts it—is the province of resource description. Historically, this work has centered on books and other printed material. Indeed, some of the terms frequently used by CMLs reflect this heritage of the printed word. Today, however, the resources we collect for our patrons exhibit a much greater variety: online books and periodicals, films and videos, musical scores, streaming media, kits, tools, and cultural artifacts like T-shirts, signs, and political buttons.

Additionally, the description of resources increasingly involves the related description of people and organizations. To help users find and identify resources, we must maintain the indexes of collections that allow collocation of and cross-references among resources in discovery interfaces; thus, it is crucial that CMLs have the ability to establish a unique identity for any person or group. In traditional cataloging, this establishment of formalized, unique names is called *authority* work. This term also encompasses the establishment of names for places and concepts. Complicating this work is the astounding proliferation of content brought about by the information age and the accompanying proliferation of the types of roles people or groups can play in creating content.

In short, the universe of discourse is immense and complex, and it is expanding. To accomplish useful description of all the types of resources and people and relationships mentioned above, we must have a reliable map of that universe. We need to name all things contained within it, define those things by type, and arrange them in relation to each other. This kind of mapping could be referred to as a data model, a reference model, a conceptual model, or a framework. Though these terms appear in different contexts and have some slightly different connotations, usually the overall goal of such models, especially within the fields of cataloging and metadata work, is to define known *entities* (resources, people, groups, places, concepts) and the *relationships* between them, usually within a specific area of knowledge.

While the Paris Principles of 1961 represent the first coordinated attempt by the international library community to draw such a map, FRBR represented the next evolution in librarianship's attempts to map the universe of discourse. As mentioned in chapter 1, FRBR was developed by IFLA and is by nature more philosophical and abstract in its modeling, which allows for its application to many different types of entities and relationships. In the FRBR map of the universe of discourse, for example, there are four types of resource entities a CML might need to describe:

Work: the essence of the resource, conceptualized in the abstract; the tune or the story or the image itself, outside of its physical or electronic embodiment.

Expression: the embodiment of the abstract work in some form; the printed text of *Jane Eyre* in English or the recording of a Puccini aria sung by Pavarotti.

Manifestation: the specific version of the expression; the Penguin Classics edition of *Jane Eyre* in English, published in 2006 with an introduction by Dr. Stevie Davis; the Kindle version of that same Penguin edition; or the Decca 2008 release of *Puccini's Greatest Arias* on CD, or the streaming version of that release offered through various services.

Item: the actual physical or electronic instance of a manifestation that your library owns, which may have its own unique characteristics that need description: an autographed copy of the 2014 edition of Volume 4 of the graphic novel *Saga* or a digitized image with certain access restrictions.

The full description of a resource might touch on all these levels, or just one or two. A traditional catalog record, for instance, has work-level information in the author and subject fields because that information relates to the nature and identity of the essential work itself. But the information in the publication statement is manifestation-level description, since the expression of a work can be manifested in many different publications or releases. If you're describing a physical resource, the call number field is often going to be an item-level description because the item may receive a slightly different shelf-address in your library than in other libraries.

In addition to helping us define the types of resource entities that exist, FRBR also defines other entities like creators and contributors, and relationships between these entities—i.e., the types of relationships person or group entities can have with resource entities, and the types of relationships that exist between resource entities. Here is breakdown of the example mentioned earlier, using the FRBR model:

- An aria is a work in itself.
- Although the aria is its own work, it is also part of a larger work (the entire opera); FRBR defines this as a whole-part relationship.
- Giacomo Puccini is the creator of both the aria (work) and the larger opera (work)
  - ☐ Usually, only creators are associated with work-level entities.
- An album of Puccini arias sung by Pavarotti comprises many works gathered together in a new expression.
  - ☐ Luciano Pavarotti is a contributor to that expression.
  - ☐ Contributors are usually only associated with expression- and manifestation-level entities (performers, publishers, editors, preface writers, translators, etc.)
- As mentioned, the release of this recording of arias on CD by Decca in 2008 is a manifestation; however, a remastered release of the same album 10 years later with a bonus track is a new manifestation, and it might have new contributors associated with it (a duet with Renee Fleming, perhaps).

Since FRBR is a high-level mapping of the universe of discourse its concepts can seem arbitrary and abstract, and new CMLs should not expect for all these terms and relationships to immediately make sense. The important thing to recognize from these examples is how useful it is to be able to systematically map out all of the important information about a resource. A framework like FRBR is crucial in descriptive work.

As further chapters of this book will illustrate, a framework is of course just the beginning. For adequate guidance, CMLs rely on many other standards, guidelines, and best practices, layered on top of such frameworks and combined with each other. This array of cataloging and metadata protocols can be overwhelming and bewildering to a new CML, so below is a breakdown of standards and their categories. This should provide a basis for the information covered here and in succeeding chapters.

Frameworks Data models Conceptual models Reference models	Abstract, high-level standards that serve as an overall mapping or model for a domain of knowledge.	FRBR, FRAD, RDF, CiDOC, LRM
Ontologies Schemas	More specific models with accompanying vocabularies that define classes of things and the properties those things can have; constructed specifically for use in linked data environments.	BIBFRAME 2.0, Schema.org, RDFS
Content standards Data content standards Descriptive standards Display standards Schemas	Standards that tell CMLs what to record about a resource, and how to record it; oriented toward creating description for human readers; usually the primary tool in descriptive work, with frameworks and encoding standards operating more in the background.	RDA, AACR2, DCRM, DACS, CCO, ISBD, Dublin Core
Encoding standards Data structure standards Data encoding standards Data exchange standards Syntax standards Content schemas	Standards that allow computers to read, store, and exchange data; think of these as containers for existing descriptive data; for instance, MARC21 provides containers for RDA descriptions created by a cataloger.	MARC21, XML, JSON-LD, METS, MODS, EAD, Turtle, N3
Controlled vocabularies Value standards Data value standards Authority files	Lists (sometimes hierarchical) of authorized terms and cross-referenceable variants for concepts, people, and places; with content standards, one of the CML's primary descriptive tools.	LCSH, NAF, LCGFT, TGM, AAT, TGN, CONA, ULAN, DCMI Type, MODS Type, MeSH, GNIS
Classification systems	Extensive knowledge organization systems designed to help physically arrange materials by category.	Library of Congress Classification, Dewey Decimal Classification

As you explore these standards more thoroughly, it will be clear that FRBR's top-level principles have been widely disseminated (though not unanimously accepted), and have trickled into practice throughout the cataloging community, and to some extent the metadata community as well. For example, the cataloging content standard Resource Description and Access (RDA), the successor to AACR2, is built on FRBR's principles, and gives practical, detailed instructions for recording information about works, expressions, manifestations, items, creators, contributors, etc. However, FRBR will soon be replaced by a revised and expanded version called the Library Reference Model (LRM). This model has updated definitions of entities and relationships which will change, to a degree, the existing mapping we just covered. As of the time of this writing, the final draft of the LRM document has undergone worldwide review and has finalized this new list of entities:

RES—the highest entity level, meaning simply "thing"

- Work
- Expression
- Manifestation
- Item
- Agent
  - Person
  - Collective agent
- Nomen
- Place
- Time-span

We won't cover the differences between FRBR and LRM in any depth here. As a new CML, you just need to know that theoretical frameworks for resource description exist, and you will need to combine a familiarity with such frameworks with more practical knowledge of the specific standards covered in chapters 3 and 4. Also, note that by 2019 LRM is expected to become the new widely accepted model for the work of description, and since the content standard RDA is so closely aligned with FRBR, revisions will be made to RDA as well.

In the meantime, CMLs are also investigating other models that could fundamentally inform the way we describe resources in the near future. One of these is Resource Description Framework (RDF), a data model for the web which outlines a structure for making statements about resources. The particular structure of RDF would allow us to build endless connections between statements, which in turn would permit machines to interpret information much more granularly than current web standards allow. To understand the kind of modeling RDF does, it's helpful to compare it to grammar. Grammar is the shared framework we all use to arrange our words in logical ways to create meaning. The RDF data model can be thought of like a grammar for the web, designed to help machines and applications "understand" the meaning of the data they process. To accomplish this, RDF tells us to structure statements into triples like so:

SUBJECT → PREDICATE → OBJECT

As you can see, this is a very open and high-level data model. RDF does of course offer more specific guidance about the nature of subjects, predicates, and objects, and provides some terms in its RDF Schema ontology (RDFS) that can be used to make statements. But largely, RDF is designed to accommodate other systems of mapping and naming. For instance, in the LAM community, we can use RDF to make statements about all the entities and relationships we've mapped out in FRBR, or LRM, or RDA, or Dublin Core, any other content standard we use for our work:

Work → has relationship to → person

Person → has relationship to → work

Charlotte Bronte → wrote → textual work Jane Eyre

Textual work *Jane Eyre* → has adaptation → 2006 BBC miniseries *Jane Eyre*

2006 BBC miniseries *Jane Eyre* → has performer → Ruth Wilson

Ruth Wilson → performed in → BBC television show *Luther*

Again, it comes down to identifying entities and describing relationships between them. It's easy to see how quickly RDF triple statements could generate an infinite constellation of entities (subjects and objects) with connections drawn between them (predicates), tracing the entire universe of discourse. Keep in mind too that RDF is an open web standard for use by any application or on any site. So while it can be adapted for describing library resources, its implementation is envisioned across the entire internet. The implications of a shared, open structure for expressing all online information are exciting. Right now, as we know, search engines don't understand our library-specific data and can't effectively access our resource descriptions—a problem whose scope cannot be overstated.

If the majority of online content were expressed using the shared grammar of RDF, it would be possible to connect the constellation of library resource description data to other constellations of internet information, and machines could travel paths through all that interconnected data like lightning. Search engines and applications could actually "read" meaning in those connections, rather than just passively relaying information for humans to interpret. Powerful visibility, accessibility, and interoperability would be possible. That is the vision of the Semantic Web, the next expected evolution of the internet. In terms of cataloging and metadata work, such an evolution would translate to serious advancements in resource discovery.

Of course, as mentioned, libraries need much more than abstract mappings or models to achieve high-quality resource description, whether in current or in future envisioned environments. Cataloging and metadata work depend upon very specific instructions and sets of authorized terms that build out from those frameworks and make them actionable in daily practice. And, as discussed below, these instructions and authorities must be widely standardized and broadly shared to be the most effective.

COOPERATIVE CATALOGING

In 1841, in his role as Keeper of Printed Books at the British Museum, Antonio Panizzi published his *Ninety-One Cataloguing Rules* in an attempt to standardize descriptive practice, essentially kickstarting professional efforts to make cataloging more consistent across libraries.

THEORETICAL PRINCIPLES OF RESOURCE DESCRIPTION **29**

But as Panizzi was to discover, finding time to generate rich, high-quality description can be a challenge for cultural institutions. Although proposed in 1841, the final printed catalog of the British Museum's books was not published in full until 1881 (Harris, 2008). Ultimately, the staff hours required for good cataloging far exceeded anyone's expectations.

In the United States, this dilemma was eventually surmounted by the development of cooperative cataloging, or shared catalog records. As standardization increased and description of resources grew more consistent, it was conceivable that a catalog record created in one library for a particular resource could easily be used in another library holding the same title. Clearly, there was no need for each library to reinvent the wheel.

With the introduction of the card catalog (a vast improvement on printed library catalogues like Panizzi's, which was out of date as soon as it reached the shelves and was difficult and expensive to revise), the Library of Congress (LC) was able to assume a central role in the production and distribution of standard catalog records via mailed cards. Of course, libraries continued to create their own local resource descriptions when no matching LC records were available. But when LC implemented the MARC exchange format in the early 1970s, it soon became possible for any institution to contribute their locally-created records to a larger pool, thus increasing the available catalog data for all libraries to draw upon.

These early advances in record sharing set the stage for today's cooperative cataloging environment, which comprises an enormous network of institutions, professional organizations, protocols, and vendor services. Cooperative cataloging now involves coordinated effort not only to create and share consistent resource descriptions (bibliographic records), but also consistent and unique identification for people, places, and concepts (authority records). The practice of searching for, editing, and downloading bibliographic records for your local institution is called *copy cataloging*, while the process of creating and contributing an entirely new record is called *original cataloging*.

Although cooperative cataloging is of primary relevance to traditional catalogers, librarians working with other metadata will find that their work often intersects with past and current cooperative cataloging practice. For instance, the Library of Congress National

Authority File (NAF) is a rich source of unique identifiers for people, groups and places, created and curated for decades by catalogers; metadata librarians often use NAF data in creating or transforming large batches of resource descriptions.

For cooperative cataloging to work effectively, central hubs for data storage and exchange must be widely available to all libraries, and some authoritative bodies must take a lead role in crafting policy and protocol. The most important players in creating and maintaining the cooperative cataloging network in the United States are OCLC and the PCC (Program for Cooperative Cataloging).

OCLC has grown from its beginnings as a purveyor of shared catalog records into a major library vendor offering a multitude of services. Perhaps its most important contribution to cooperative cataloging is the shared WorldCat database, which comprises millions of catalog records from institutions all over the world. Subscribing institutions may both pull records from and contribute them to the WorldCat database. All records in the database are subjected to numerous quality control measures, matching and deduplication algorithms, and programmatic enhancements to stay in step with the evolution of cataloging practice. Additionally, WorldCat maintains local holdings for each subscribing institution, which promotes a number of helpful functions like inventory management, collection exposure, and interlibrary lending.

Chapter 3 will go into detail about all the data points required for an accurate and consistent catalog record, but each record contributed to WorldCat must meet a minimal encoding standard to be acceptable. Furthermore, to maintain the quality and usefulness of such an enormous database, OCLC subscribers must adhere to WorldCat's "master record" approach. Obviously, it is important to have as few duplicates as possible in the WorldCat database to promote efficiency and prevent onerous searching and matching for copy catalogers. So in principle, there should be one master record for each unique instance of a resource (or each manifestation, in FRBR terms). Catalogers should edit and correct errors in this master record to make it acceptable for use in their local institution, rather than create an entirely new record if the existing one is not adequate.

Because so many institutions are OCLC subscribers, these World-Cat database quality considerations have helped to shape larger cooperative cataloging protocols and the use of certain MARC fields.

For instance, the fixed fields in a MARC record include a field for "Encoding Level," and contain codes defined by OCLC to indicate whether the cataloging in that record is full-level, minimal-level, core-level, etc. Chapter 4 of OCLC's *Bibliographic Formats and Standards* document[1] offers guidance about what kinds of differences between a resource and a related record warrant the creation of a new master record, and though these guidelines were originally written to apply only to records contributed to WorldCat, they have assumed a more generalized authority in cataloging practice and offer useful metrics for any cataloger trying to match a record to a resource, regardless of whether their library subscribes to OCLC.

Of course, catalogers need a way to interact with the records in WorldCat; they must be able to search the database, edit records they find, or create entirely new records to contribute, which is what the software application called Connexion is used for. If your new position mostly involves traditional cataloging, you will most likely be using Connexion and the WorldCat database for your work.

However, though OCLC holds the clear monopoly in this area, other shared bibliographic databases and cataloging clients exist. Innovative's SkyRiver database and accompanying cataloging client have the largest customer base after OCLC, and it is conceivable that other vendors and services for cooperative cataloging could emerge as cataloging practice evolves.

While OCLC provides the primary logistical means for libraries to participate in the cooperative cataloging network, the Library of Congress' Program for Cooperative Cataloging (PCC) is the authoritative body behind most of its standardized protocols. Although LC is not technically a national library, its cataloging practices have set precedent for most institutions in the United States for decades due to its development of the widely-used Library of Congress Classification system (LCC) and its early role in shared catalog record distribution. As more and more libraries looked to LC for guidance, the PCC was established to oversee cooperative cataloging efforts. Essentially, its purpose is to set forth a minimum quality standard for bibliographic and authority record creation so that certain records can be marked as PCC-compliant. This work is done in cooperation with OCLC which provides the means to contribute, mark, revise, and share PCC bibliographic and authority records. It is important to note that while *bibliographic* master records can be contributed to OCLC without having to meet PCC standards, this is not true of authority records. Since LC maintains the entire file of authorized names and subjects, any new term contributed to that file (and ultimately OCLC) must comply with PCC standards.

Any library can become a member of the PCC and contribute PCC-compliant records to the WorldCat database and/or to LC's authority files, provided at least some of their catalogers complete training in PCC standards and conventions. There are four major areas of standardized practice in which catalogers can participate:

> **BIBCO:** BIBliographic COoperative; the minimum standard for monographic bibliographic records

> **CONSER:** Cooperative ONline SERials; the minimum standard for serial bibliographic records

> **NACO:** Name Authority COoperative; the minimum standard for the creation of name authority records, which may include people, groups, and places

> **SACO:** Subject Authority COoperative; for the creation of subject authority records, which may also include genre/form terms

Most large research institutions participate in the PCC, so if your position involves cataloging at an academic library you will likely need to undergo PCC training in one or more of these areas. However, many public and special libraries are also PCC members, especially when their specialized collections require subject and authority records that would not otherwise be available unless their own catalogers create them.

Initial training in these areas is coordinated by the PCC, and then further individual review of PCC submissions is conducted by catalogers at PCC member institutions. For instance, to participate in NACO you must first undergo the official NACO training from LC and then practice NACO record creation in partnership with a designated NACO reviewer from a member library who will assess each record you create and provide feedback. Once you have reached proficiency in creating NACO records, your reviewer will inform the PCC, and your institution will be granted NACO independence (i.e., the authorization to contribute NACO records directly to the LC authority file without prior review).

In each of these four areas of standardized practice the basic process may differ slightly, but the ultimate goal is to familiarize the cataloger with the minimum PCC standard and give them the tools for contributing PCC-compliant records. In each area, manuals and documentation are available to guide the cataloger in understanding and adhering to specific PCC requirements. At each American Library Association (ALA) conference, the PCC holds community meetings for all participants to share updates and take feedback, and at certain times throughout the year its subdivisions and various committees meet to discuss changes to practice and plans for the future. If your library is a PCC participant, it is important to follow these updates.

Of course, many other library-related groups and vendors have ties to the cooperative cataloging world. Many vendors offer shelf-ready programs, which include batch searching of OCLC or other databases and delivery of catalog records that match the resources ordered from the vendor. The existence of such programs is predicated on the availability of shared and properly-encoded records.

In addition, professional library organizations play a role in supporting OCLC and PCC cooperative cataloging work, and also help to set further agreed-upon conventions and best practices to promote shared record quality and consistency. The Association for Library Collections and Technical Services (ALCTS), division of ALA, is home to many committees and subcommittees tasked with reviewing and contributing to cooperative cataloging protocol. ALCTS also authored the *Differences Between, Changes Within* document,[2] which provides catalogers guidance on when to use an existing record and when to create a new one. This document is in fact cited in the previously mentioned Chapter 4 of OCLC's *Bibliographic Formats*, and should be used in tandem with OCLC's guidelines on this topic.

In the case of special formats like film and music, organizations like Online Audiovisual Catalogers (OLAC) and the Music Library Association's Bibliographic Control Committee (MLA-BCC) have developed highly detailed cataloging best practices that help catalogers consistently address the kinds of unique descriptive requirements that arise with these formats. All of this work is in support of coordinated efforts toward standardized resource description that can be shared, re-used, enhanced, and edited by an entire national community. In turn, this makes it possible for libraries to amass high-quality catalog data without overtaxing their own time and resources, while still providing optimum discoverability and access for their patrons.

REFERENCES

Alston, R. C., & Jannetta, M. J. (1978). *Bibliography, machine readable cataloguing, and the ESTC.* London: British Library.

Denton, W. (2007). FRBR and the History of Cataloging. A.E. Taylor, *Understanding FRBR: What It Is and How It Will Affect Our Retrieval Tools.* Libraries Unlimited.

Harris, P. (2008, January). *Panizzi, Sir Anthony (1797–1879).* Retrieved March 2014, from Oxford Dictionary of National Biography: www.oxforddnb .com/view/article/21231.

Olson, H. A. (2002). *The power to name: Locating the limits of subject representation in libraries.* Dordrecht, The Netherlands: Kluwer Academic Publishers.

Strout, R. F. (1956). The development of the catalog and cataloging codes. *The Library Quarterly,* 21(1), pp. 254-275.

Taylor, Arlene G. & Joudrey, Daniel N. (2009). *The organization of information.* Westport, Connecticut: Libraries Unlimited.

NOTES

1. OCLC, Bibliographic Formats and Standards, www.oclc.org/bibformats/ en.html.

2. Association for Library Collections & Technical Services, Differences Between, Changes Within: Guidelines on When to Create a New Record, 2007, www.ala.org/alcts/sites/ala.org.alcts/files/content/resources/org/ cat/differences07.pdf.

CHAPTER THREE

Learning
the Standards
Cataloging

In previous chapters we have looked at cataloging and metadata management as it relates to users and information retrieval systems (Chapter 1), and at the theoretical underpinnings of information management (Chapter 2). In this chapter we will dive into the process of metadata creation itself—descriptive and access metadata—and take a closer look at the types of information CMLs record.

DESCRIPTION AND ACCESS

Description

Bibliographic description consists of recording basic information about what a given resource *looks like* (its physical details), and transcribing, where appropriate, the words used and resource uses to describe itself, such as title, the name of the author, and so forth. This information is gathered together into a set sequence and forms a core around which other metadata elements (access points and subject access points) can be arranged. The chief purpose of this information is to enable users to *identify* the resource being described to establish a reliable association between the resource represented in the discovery environment, and the resource that exists in the institution's collection.

The specific types of information needed to identify a resource successfully depends, to a certain degree, on the type of resource being collected. However, the information typically falls under these general categories:

> **Title:** What is the resource called? The title or titles used to refer to the resource.
>
> **Responsibility:** What are the names of the individuals and/ or organizations that contributed to the creation of this resource, and what are their roles?
>
> **Edition:** Some resources, such as monographs, appear in various slightly different versions under the same title. In these instances, is it helpful to record information that identifies the specific version (or edition).
>
> **Publication or production:** Where, by whom, and when was this resource published? Or if this is an unpublished resource, what were the circumstances of its production? This information can play an important role in facilitating the identification of specific resources.
>
> **Series information:** In cases where a resource has been issued as part of a larger group or set of resources, this information aids in identification.
>
> The basic **physical attributes** of the resource. Exactly what attributes are to be recorded depends on the particular type or format. Typically, however, the size or duration of the resource, format-specific details such as whether it is illustrated or not, and the resources physical dimensions (if it has any), are considered descriptively significant.
>
> Any **standard identifiers** (such as ISBN) that may appear on or associated with the resource.
>
> **Location** or **access:** Information that enables users to get their hands on the resource, or get the resource onto their

screens, as the case may be. Typically this is, for physical resources, a call number or other collection arrangement device, and for digital resources, either a URL, or more commonly, a link to some kind of access-mediation service (such as link resolver or knowledgebase, etc.) that provides user access to digital resources.

A key principle of descriptive metadata practice is that the information that CMLs gather is based on identifiable **sources of information.** Whenever possible, we want to derive descriptive information from the resource being described, rather than relying on second-hand accounts (such as bibliographies or publisher catalogs).

For many types of resources, it is not enough to know that the information comes from the resource itself, but we also want to know the specific location on the resource where it was found. Take a book, for example. Most (though certainly not all) books have title pages that present the title and author to the reader; information about the publication of the book (the "imprint') is also a common feature of title pages. But this information may also appear on other locations on the book, such as the cover or the spine. In order to manage this complexity and ensure that they are all on the same page (pun intended), CMLs have developed shared understandings of where on a book to look first for title information and where else to look should the title page not be found.

Of course the world is far from perfect, and it is not always possible to find all of the necessary descriptive information about a resource on the resource itself. Compare our book with a handwritten letter, which may only contain oblique signs of its author, publication date, and so forth; it is likely to lack a title altogether. In cases like these, other sources of information—such as references works, publishers' catalogs, and websites—might be needed. In extreme cases, necessary information might just not be available to the cataloger at all, and they will need to supply something based on what is known about its origin and/or provenance, or simply a descriptive epithet. In most cases where necessary information is not found on the resource but instead drawn out of some external source, that information is marked (usually by enclosing it in brackets [thus]) so that users are made aware of its extrinsic nature.

Access

Not all of the descriptive information that CMLs record interests users directly. It would be extremely unlikely (though not of course completely impossible) for a user to enter a library and ask to see all the books that are 400 pages long, or twenty-eight centimeters tall, or that were published in New York. This information may prove critical to users later when they want to *select* among various results the item that meets their specific needs; but most users, seeking to find resources of interest, focus primarily on what resources are called (titles), who they were created by (authors, publishers, and contributors), or what they are about (subjects, genres, etc.) While most of the information needed to answer these types of questions is present in the descriptive information, because that information is derived from the bibliographic resources themselves, it may not be presented to the user in a very useful manner. In order to provide better answers we must move beyond simply recording descriptive information to providing and controlling access points (APs).

What do we mean by "access point"? An access point (sometimes called a "heading") is a fixed and unique string that enables users to *find*, *identify*, and *select* entities that are relevant to the resource being described. This can include the names of associated individuals (authors, editors, illustrators); organizations (publishers, sponsors, hosts); artistic or literary works, places, topics, concepts; and others. All APs are designed to be a controlled way to retrieve resources; a preferred form of the name of the entity is chosen and used consistently, and variants are often recorded to redirect users to the preferred form.

Names

Authorship—the role of a resource's creator—is the most common relationship that is recorded through an AP, and a good place to start for investigating how APs work. Like descriptive information, access metadata is derived from the resources themselves. However, in order to provide users a single, unique, and identifiable access point for each entity in the catalog or discovery environment, CMLs must take into account a wider array of bibliographic facts than just what can be found on a single resource.

As an example, let's look at the way Ursula K. Le Guin (1929–2018) would be represented as an access point in a catalog or discovery environment. On the vast majority of her published works her name appears as "Ursula K. Le Guin." On a few, however, it appears without the middle initial: "Ursula Le Guin." This difference is small enough to go virtually unnoticed by readers. If we were generating an index of authors based solely on how their names appear on the title pages of their published works we would end up with two separate entries:

> Le Guin, Ursula

> Le Guin, Ursula K.

A user looking for everything by Le Guin should not have to know or care whether her middle initial appears on the title page. They expect to find all of the works by the author in a single place. Knowing that these two presentations of the name are equivalent, a CML will choose the form of name that appears the most recognizable to users. This is called the "preferred name" and will form the basis of the access point going forward. So in our example, seeing as the form with the middle initial is, by an order of magnitude, more prevalent among the author's published works, the CML would select "Le Guin, Ursula K." as the preferred name. At the same time, known or surmised variants are identified and will form the basis of any variant access points (VAP).

Access Points

Selecting and recording the preferred name is the first step toward creating an AP. By doing so, the CML ensures that all works by an individual (or organization) are *collocated*—that is to say, logically brought together in one place (an index or a set of query results) for users to inspect. In many cases the name alone will be the final AP. But, in other cases, additional information needs to be added to this name. Access metadata not only collocates variants together under a single AP, it also distinguishes that AP from every other in the environment. This means that access points often consist of not just names but additional bits of information that serve to ensure that a name is unique relative to other names or to help users identify the person (or, associate the person in their heads with the one who appears in the discovery environment).

Most music libraries will have works by three Viennese composers named Johann Strauss. The most famous is certainly Johann

Strauss, Jr. (1825–1899), composer of the celebrated Blue Danube Waltz (1866). Strauss's father and nephew, also named Johann Strauss, were active composers in their own rights. While this is perhaps interesting enough to show up in a pub quiz, for a catalog or discovery environment, it presents a challenge. In order to distinguish the three composers who all have the same *preferred name* as three separate, identifiable APs, we must add *qualifying* information—in this case, biographical dates—to each:

> Strauss, Johann, 1804–1849
>
> Strauss, Johann, 1825–1899
>
> Strauss, Johann, 1866–1939

While birth and death dates are one of the most reliable ways of guaranteeing a name becomes a unique and identifiable access point, in some situations CMLs will need to rely on other methods of qualifying (that is, adding to) a name to transform it into a full-unique access point. Dates associated with an individual are often not publicly available, or (if it is someone from the past) may be unknown entirely. In some cases, the fuller form of an author's name can be added even though it appears as a set of initials on that person's published works.

> Johnson, B. (Brann)
>
> Johnson, B. (Brett)

If this information is also not available, as the case may be, a brief descriptive characterization of the individual's profession, or other identifying characteristic, can be used:

> Johnson, Bill (Film editor)
>
> Johnson, Bill (Jazz musician)
>
> Johnson, Bill (Playwright)

In some cases, a combination of these qualifiers may be used to provide a unique and identifiable point of access for an individual or organization.

Before we move on: remember how, when a CML chooses a preferred name, she also identifies other forms as variants? These variant names can be treated in a manner similar to preferred names to form *variant access points* (VAPs). VAPs function to direct users to the AAP; in many systems the VAP will appear in indexes as a "*see*" reference:

> Le Guin, Ursula, 1929–2018 *see* Le Guin, Ursula K., 1929–2018
>
> Guin, Ursula Le, 1929–2018 *see* Le Guin, Ursula K., 1929–2018
>
> Kroeber, Ursula, 1929–2018 *see* Le Guin, Ursula K., 1929–2018

One important difference between an authorized AP and a variant AP is that there is no systematic requirement that VAPs be unique. Since their primary function is essentially to serve as signposts directing traffic to their respective AAPs, it is ok—perhaps even preferable—to have multiple variants of the same form.

> ALA, *see*
>
> > American Library Association
> >
> > American Lung Association
> >
> > Association of Laboratory Automation

Subjects

As mentioned, personal names aren't the only types of APs catalogers include in resource descriptions. The name of a related work may be an access point or the name of a conference or corporation. These APs are established in much the same manner using a preferred form and its variants.

In most cases, it's easy for the CML to quickly identify associated people or groups or places, and either locate or construct a unique AP for those entities. Subjects are a different matter, however. A resource doesn't immediately reveal to you what it is about. Although there are plenty of controlled vocabulary terms available for use as subject APs, the CML must perform some extra evaluation and decision-making before they can even choose these terms. This process is called subject analysis and involves a robust but efficient survey of the resource's nature and content. This is, without doubt, a complex domain: entire books have been written about this step of resource description alone.[1] This section seeks to give you a grounding in the basics and equip you to explore further.

To perform subject analysis, here is a basic set of steps to follow:

- Locate keywords from one or all of the following:
  - ☐ Title and subtitle
  - ☐ Publishers' summary
  - ☐ Table of contents
  - ☐ Foreword, introduction, etc.
- Working from your keywords, ask yourself these questions:
  - ☐ Which concept or concepts predominate?
  - ☐ What subtopics are also reflected? Are they important enough to include?
  - ☐ How specific can I get with each of the most important terms I've identified?
  - ☐ If I were a patron, what terms would I find most helpful and/or relevant in discovering this resource? Is there a term I'm missing that would seem obvious to a patron?

Be aware as you perform this survey that your subject choices will also form the basis for classification of the resource (outlined in more detail below). It's also important to note that this survey is usually only applicable for non-fiction resources; historically, works of fiction, drama, etc., received very little subject treatment from catalogers. This is changing and works of fiction now frequently receive subject headings when broad themes are easily identifiable, but usually your survey of a fiction resource will still be much more general and abbreviated.

Once you complete this survey, you will choose terms from various controlled vocabularies available to you to serve as the subject APs in your resource description. See the section on Library of Congress Subject Headings in the following pages for more details.

Authorities

This discussion of how and why authorized access points are constructed raises another question: where does this additional information about individuals and organizations reside in an information retrieval system? It does not make a lot of sense to repeat this information in each bibliographic description of each of Ursula Le Guin's published works. For this reason, most information retrieval systems use some form of "authorities file" or other "authority control" system. Simply put, an authorities file is a separate, related file of information, which is designed to enable the identification of the entities (authors and organizations, for example) that are relevant to the resources in the "bibliographic file," that is, the catalog of information resources.

Each entity in an authorities file has its own *name authority record* (NAR). The NAR typically contains the following information: (a) the *authorized access point* for the entity; (b) any *variant access points* for the entity; (c) significant relationships between that entity and other entities in the authority file; (d) other useful identifying information about that entity (such as dates of biographical significance, descriptors, biographical notes, etc.); and finally, (e) brief references to the sources of information that support all of the above. It is important to note here that like descriptive information the information recorded in authority records is based on known, publicly available sources. This includes the resources themselves (for example, a name that appears on a title page) as well as other published reference sources and other forms of communication such as correspondence. These sources of information are recorded in the NAR so others can evaluate the information presented in the record accurately.

An authorities file often provides a companion resource to the catalog or information retrieval system it governs. Since its primary purpose is to facilitate the management of access points in the bibliographic file itself, the authorities files of many libraries are not publicly available, or only appear to users through the indexes that they help to organize. However, recently this information has been viewed by some as useful and interesting in its own right; and some authorities files and resources based on authorities metadata have been made available to the public.[2]

A Critical Approach to Subject and Identity Metadata

Before we move on it is worth noting that libraries have long positioned themselves as neutral and disinterested arbiters of the information they collect and the services they provide. Our professional standards and ethics have been built around the shared principles of universality and freedom of expression.[3] While these principles themselves are not in doubt, many have asked the question of whether they are achieved through an assumed position of "neutrality." Are libraries, and other information-centered institutions, truly acting as neutral parties or—in a world that is inevitably defined by resource constraints—do the choices these institutions make about what they collect (and do not collect) reflect values and biases of their own? If libraries are excluding voices and perspectives through implicit or in some cases explicit institutional biases, can they really be said to be serving the goal of "every reader has their book"? If libraries can set aside, or at least question, the assumption of neutrality, it may be easier to detect such biases and address them.

Cataloging and metadata management has likewise often approached controlled names, subjects, and their management from an ostensibly neutral position. The tools we use, and much of the discourse around our profession, assume a degree of objectivity about bibliographic facts; for example, catalogers do not attempt to evaluate whether a resource is "good" or "bad" (morally or substantively), they focus on characterizing what it is "about" and finding relevant terms in the subject thesaurus. When we choose a preferred form of someone's name we look to the resources they have published and to biographical facts about them.

And yet the question of the overall neutrality involved in the act of assigning metadata is inescapable: when we communicate through the medium of the catalog that a certain resource is "about" something, we confer an institutional claim of value to both the resource, and the term(s) used to describe it. When we maintain a category of material for users to browse through, we reify and reinforce that category's existence in the user's mental map of the universe. Therefore, we need to pay attention to the slow, ongoing process of subject and category creation in which we are (whether we acknowledge it or not) participants.

Likewise, when we choose an authorized form of someone's name and create an authority record with personal information like birthdate and gender, we are on some level defining that person's identity. This process, although seemingly fact-based, can have implications of power and bias that CMLs should learn to consider. For instance, what of authors of zines whose names may appear on what they considered underground publications, and who may not wish to be identified at all in a library's public catalog?

As conversations and perspectives around this topic continue to expand in the professional community, we recognize now that simple "neutrality" is neither an achievable nor a desirable goal, and we're better off acknowledging from the start that all of our work can be affected by inherent and often unexplored cultural and social perspectives. You will not find in this volume the solutions to the problems, or answers to the questions surrounding neutrality, objectivity, and the values librarians hold. There are entire works outlining the many issues here and we encourage you to explore this crucial topic, keep a critical eye on the tools catalogers use as you train, and find ways to participate in ongoing professional conversations.[4]

SUMMARY

To review, "description" and "access" represent two different types of metadata that relate to each other in important ways. Access points provide users with the ability to ask complex questions about the resources in a collection, while the underlying descriptive information ensures that the answers to these queries are bibliographically precise and useful. One is not more or less important than the other; it is no accident that the current form of cataloging instructions is called *Resource Description and Access (RDA)*. Description provides a basis of information about resources, while assigning and managing access points mediates that descriptive information in ways useful to users and systems. The two work together to ensure accuracy and discoverability of large and diverse collections.

In the following table, the basic elements of descriptive and access point metadata are summarized.

ELEMENT	DESCRIPTION	ACCESS
Title	Title on piece being cataloged [= Title of the work, usually]	
Other titles	Other titles on the piece (cover, e.g.)	Other titles of the work (translated title, e.g.)
Authors	Statement of responsibility (SoR) on the piece	APs for author(s). Main AP for primary or first-named; added APs for all other contributors.
Edition	Edition statement on piece being cataloged	
Publication	Place, name of publisher, date of publication, etc.	APs for publisher or issuing body
Physical description	Length/duration, details, dimensions, etc.	
Series	Series statement on piece	AAP for series
Subject, topic, genre	Abstracts or summaries	Subject APs (SAPs), form/genre APs Classification
Standard identifiers	ISBN, etc. as appears on piece	Standard identifiers (both physical and digital)

CURRENT STANDARDS

As introduced in Chapter 2, catalogers use a number of standards to create, format, and encode the descriptive data and access points for resources; these standards govern the entire descriptive process, from describing the resource's attributes, associated agents, and subjects all the way through classification and shelflisting.

This highly regulated approach to descriptive work is crucial for a number of reasons. Machines must be able to store, index, search, and display descriptive data, of course, because users rely on these automatic machine functions for discovery. But users also rely on consistency in the human-readable display for easy comprehension.

Much of this display is controlled by the particular system your library uses, but the actual formatting and grammar of the text strings in your catalog records matters as well. If you searched your library catalog for resources about climate change and each record you found used different wording or recorded different aspects about the resource, you would have a difficult time choosing between resources. In other words, adherence to standards creates consistency and consistency creates discoverability.

The following are the standards you will need to get started. More formal training is beneficial, and we provide suggestions for those in Chapter 6, along with detailed listings of all the specific tools you need to do this work.

RDA (Content standard)

A content standard is generally where the CML begins because it tells them which attributes of the resource should be described and how that description should be formatted and arranged. For instance, a content standard might tell you to record the physical characteristics of the resource and give you guidance on measuring or identifying those characteristics (record CD size in inches, record book size in centimeters, etc.). Additionally, content standards in cataloging give guidance about describing people or groups associated with resources. In other words, the content standard will generally guide you in providing both description and access points for the resource.

Until 2013, AACR2 was the primary content standard in use for traditional cataloging. After the implementation of RDA by the Library of Congress in 2013, most other libraries followed suit and are now performing all their original cataloging under RDA. As the cooperative cataloging network permeates every library's operations, even libraries that haven't officially adopted RDA are acquiring and displaying RDA records in their catalogs.

RDA arranges its instructions in different sections that address description of (W) works, (E) expressions, (M) manifestations, and (I) items, as well as the description of agents (people associated with resources), and the description of the types of relationships that can exist between agents and resources. As outlined in Chapter 2, the WEMI entities represent resources at various intellectual levels. The original language of the work *Jane Eyre* is English; that is a work-level attribute. A Spanish translation of *Jane Eyre* is an expression of the original work; entering the MARC code for the Spanish language into your catalog record is expression-level information.

RDA guides you in understanding what information should be recorded at each WEMI-entity level and how it should be recorded. Each section is subdivided into more granular sets of instructions which address specific issues of description. For example, the subsection about recording the publication date of a manifestation offers guidance on what language to include in the catalog record if no publication date is evident on the resource, and how to record a range of dates.

For a more specific example, here is an excerpt from the RDA section about identifying the preferred names of persons, which must be done when establishing access points:

Preferred name for a person

Sources of information

Determine a preferred name for person from the following sources (in order of preference):

a) the preferred sources of information (see 2.2.2) in manifestations associated with the person
b) other formal statements appearing in manifestations associated with the person
c) other sources (including reference sources)

When a name of person appears in more than one language, see additional instructions at 9.2.2.5.2.

When the name is found in a script that differs from a preferred script of the agency creating the data, see 9.2.2.5.3.

By its nature, RDA is lengthy and highly detailed; as you can see, references to other areas of RDA are frequent and can often lead the cataloger on a merry dance through related points of information. Navigating through RDA's many sections or finding guidance on a specific point isn't always intuitive. Allow yourself time and hands-on practice to become familiar with locating, interpreting, and applying RDA's instructions.

The first version of RDA was published in 2010 as a joint effort of the American Library Association (ALA), Canadian Library Association (CLA), and the Chartered Institute of Library and Information

Professionals (CILIP), a United Kingdom organization. Maintenance of and upkeep for the official RDA standard is governed by the RDA Steering Committee (RSC), a body of professional librarians which considers proposals from the cataloging community and is responsible for making and releasing periodic updates to RDA's content. Many working groups, committees, and subcommittees throughout professional cataloging organizations work in collaboration with the RSC on matters of update and revision. The RSC is undergoing a transition to a new international governance structure which will be implemented in 2019.

The latest print version of RDA will be available in 2018, but most catalogers' institutions subscribe to the online version of RDA, currently called the RDA Toolkit.[5] There is a cost for either version, as there was a cost for purchasing access to AACR2 in previous years. Most libraries view these as routine fees for essential tools, though some concern has been voiced about the cost of access to cooperative cataloging standards for smaller libraries with few resources. If your institution is struggling to afford access to RDA, join the cataloging email lists detailed in Chapter 6 and reach out to catalogers at other institutions for assistance and recommendations. You can also turn to freely available conference presentations and archived webinars for some additional education.

As a reminder, FRBR is the underlying framework that RDA is built on, and the adoption of LRM as the successor to FRBR in 2017 means that some RDA guidelines are undergoing revision. In conjunction, the RSC decided it was a good time to make some other significant changes to the Toolkit's structure and design. The numbered rules cited in the RDA excerpt above will no longer be accurate because of the extent of restructuring and reorganizing taking place (Be sure to keep this in mind when you are viewing other older RDA training materials!). All these changes are expected to be finalized in 2019. For this reason especially, catalogers will find it most useful to use the online version of RDA; this will allow you to remain current regardless of how many updates come down the pike in the near future.

The Association for Library Collections & Technical Services (ALCTS) webinar archive[6] is a great place to find free and fairly recent RDA training webinars like "RDA for Copy Catalogers: The Basics" presented by Vicki Sipe in February 2015. For training opportunities with a cost, regional organizations are usually a good bet.

For instance, Midwest Library Collaborative Services (MCLS) offers periodic online RDA training courses at decent prices. Older and freely available presentations about the differences between RDA and AACR2 are plentiful and useful to peruse as well; though RDA has been revised significantly since its first release in 2010, you will find it helpful to be conversant in these differences as you encounter AACR2 and AACR2-RDA hybrid records in your daily work.

ISBD (Content Standard)

ISBD is a standard for formatting bibliographic description that works in tandem with RDA and was also used in conjunction with AACR2. While RDA and AACR2 instruct catalogers on the particulars of what details to record about a resource, ISBD focuses more on the actual formatting and punctuation of that written information.

One of the primary benefits of ISBD to the cataloging community was that it enabled precise arrangement of text on and printing of catalog cards so that machines could consistently produce cards and users' eyes could go to the same spot on the card every time and expect to see the same content.

In combination with MARC field tags and delimiters, ISBD punctuation in catalog records brings some of the same consistency to online catalog record display. However, some in the cataloging community feel ISBD punctuation is less necessary now in these online discovery environments, and proposals to abandon use of ISBD have been considered. Regardless of ISBD's uncertain future in cataloging work, you will need to know the basics of ISBD punctuation to create catalog records in the present environment.

The full ISBD standard is available in print, but probably not a necessary investment. There will be sufficient examples of ISBD punctuation in other cataloging training materials, the OCLC Bibliographic Formats reference website, and in the hundreds of catalog records you will soon be reviewing. In the meantime, here is a basic example of some ISBD punctuation elements that are always included in catalog records (Note that in addition to punctuation elements, ISBD also requires a particular type of spacing.):

Title : subtitle/statement of responsibility.

Place of publication : Publisher, YYYY.

Extent of resource : illustration information ; size of resource.

If you have worked in libraries for any length of time, this arrangement of information probably looks very familiar to you. ISBD
also governs the use of periods at the end of most MARC fields,
the arrangement of information about series, and so forth. You will
quickly become familiar with all these conventions as you progress
in your cataloging training.

Other Content Standards

RDA and ISBD guide much of cataloging work, but if you are
cataloging archival or rare materials you may work more with
content standards like *Describing Archives: A Content Standard*
(DACS) or *Descriptive Cataloging of Rare Materials* (DCRM).

DACS is governed by the Society of American Archivists (SAA)
and based on the same FRBR principles as RDA. It deals with
the description of all types of archival materials and the special
considerations they require, including conditions of access, sources
of acquisition, etc. The latest edition of DACS is available for free
online.[7]

DCRM is governed by the Rare Books and Manuscript Section
(RBMS), which is both a section of the Association of College &
Research Libraries (ACRL) and a division of ALA. RBMS maintains
several different variations of DCRM for formats like books
(DCRM(B)), serials (DCRM(S)), graphic materials (DCRM(G)), and
others. These guides address description of the unique qualities of
rare materials and are available as free PDFs[8] on the RBMS website.
Unlike DACS, which is a comprehensive standard, DCRM was
designed to work in conjunction with AACR2, and has not yet been
brought fully into alignment with RDA. In the meantime, special
instructions are provided for catalogers wishing to create RDA-
compliant DCRM records.[9]

LCSH (Controlled Vocabulary)

Once you have completed the subject analysis process covered
previously, it's time to choose a value standard from which to pull
authorized vocabulary terms that reflect your identified concepts. In
most cases, that standard is going to be Library of Congress Subject
Headings (LCSH), though the nature of your institution and specific
job position may have you working with vocabularies like the Art &
Architecture Thesaurus (AAT), the Thesaurus for Graphic Materials

(TGM), or any number of other such thesauri employed across libraries, archives, and museums.

All these vocabularies have their own structures and guidelines for application. LCSH, for example, has rules that instruct the cataloger to choose terms at the highest level of specificity available, and to only assign terms to concepts that represent 20 percent or more of the resource's content. There are further (and increasingly complex) rules about the construction of subject heading strings since LCSH allows catalogers to append subdivisions to an initial term to reflect sub-topical, geographical, chronological, or form information like so:

```
650 _0 Counterculture $z Chile $x History $y 20th
       century $v Pictorial works.
```

This kind of subject string of terms accomplishes what is called precoordination: the pulling together of multiple related terms to form one highly specific concept. Some vocabularies are designed for precoordination, while others prefer a post-coordinated approach in which single terms are applied separately and exist independently from each other.

The full LCSH hierarchical vocabulary is available through Classification Web,[10] a subscription that your department should already have if LCSH is the primary means for subject description at your library. Learning to navigate the LCSH vocabulary and the many rules for its application will take time and practice. Library of Congress provides a free, in-depth, online training that is an excellent place to start.[11]

FAST and Other Faceted Vocabularies

A further note about pre-coordination vs. post-coordination: Much debate exists on which of these approaches is better because either choice impacts search interface features and behavior and thus the patron discovery experience.

In fact, OCLC has recently implemented an automatic program called Faceted Application of Subject Terminology (FAST) that breaks down pre-coordinated LCSH strings into individual terms;[12]

this in turn allows their WorldCat discovery interface to offer patrons a faceted subject search wherein results for a very broad search can then be narrowed down by clicking on various available facets. Other libraries can also choose to use these FAST headings in their local systems, if they wish. So as a new cataloger you'll want to pay attention to the pre-coordination versus post-coordination discussion, on both the local and national level.

LCGFT (Controlled Vocabulary)

When you have finished subject analysis, you will also want to examine the genre or form of the item and use appropriate value standards to reflect that information as well. The time-honored cataloger mantra tells us that while the subject is what the resource is *about*, the genre and form should reflect what the resource *is* (this is why you will often will hear the manufactured terms "aboutness" and "is-ness" in the cataloging community). In other words, a resource may be *about* maternal health in Kenya, but it *is* a documentary film. So you might assign the terms:

```
650 _0 Maternal health services $z Kenya
655 _7 Documentary films $2 lcdgt
```

The second term is taken from LC's Genre/Form Term vocabulary (LCGFT), another value standard that catalogers use frequently. As with LCSH, the LCGFT vocabulary is available in Classification Web and is accompanied by instructions for use and application that you should become familiar with. You will also note that both LCSH and LCGFT terms receive a specific type of MARC coding so our library systems can index and display them properly (you will see further examples in the MARC section below).

Other LC Controlled Vocabularies

As you start exploring LC thesauri, you'll discover that even more exist: the Medium of Performance Terms (LCMPT) for music and the Demographic Group Terms (LCDGT) for indicating the demographic characteristics of the creator or intended audience. You only need to concern yourself with the LCMPT if you know music cataloging will be among your responsibilities, in which case you'll need not only familiarity with LCMPT but another entire set of specialized cataloging skills (this additional layer of expertise is often needed with any type of special format, from cartographic materials to rare books to audiovisual resources—see Chapter 5 for more details). The LCDGT is a relatively new vocabulary and many institutions haven't incorporated its use in routine practice; as a new cataloger, keep a weather eye out for developments on this front, and perhaps check out the LCDGT draft manual[13] in the meantime. And of course, there are many other subject and genre value standards for you to explore, as your time and work guide you.

Ultimately, every experienced cataloger develops their own routines for this stage of descriptive work—one that efficiently combines familiarity with a set of vocabularies with a thorough and thoughtful examination of the resource, all while avoiding too much agonizing. Remember that you are not expected to be an expert on every topic and concept out there, and that whatever subject access you can responsibly provide is helpful for the user.

Classification and Shelflisting

Even in this age of widespread digital publication and collection, most libraries and other document-centered institutions still hold, and continue to acquire, print and other tangible material. For these collections the question of where to put all of their stuff, in order to ensure that their users (not to mention their own staff) can retrieve their selected resources quickly and reliably, remains an important one. Beyond expedience, many institutions see the value in maintaining an ordered physical arrangement of their print resources to help their users discover resources that might be relevant to their interests. Although the catalog or information retrieval system, ideally, provides a holistic and user-focused view of a library's collections, users and librarians alike continue to enjoy and value the serendipity of browsing stacks that have been systematically arranged by topic or genre.

Location of materials is usually divided into two separate procedures. "Classification" is the first and involves supplying a code or address for a resource, usually based on its topic or discipline.

The goal of classification is thus to collocate, or bring together, all resources in a given collection according to their overall topic: history with history, science with science, and so forth. Once a resource has been classified, the CML will typically assign a unique address (or call number) to the work: this second process is called "shelflisting."

Classification systems

There is no such thing as a universal classification system as different institutions use different methods of organizing their resources on a topical level. The choice of which classification system to use is typically made for the whole collection (though it is not unheard of for libraries to support multiple classification systems, typically for legacy reasons) and greatly depends on the institution's user base and resource needs. Two classification systems are in widespread use in North America.

Dewey

The Dewey Decimal Classification System (DDC) was created by Melville Dewey (1851–1931) in 1876 and has been in continuous revision and use by American libraries ever since. DDC is based on dividing the world of topical disciplines into a universal hierarchy and placing each resource on an appropriate branch of that hierarchy.

DDC employs a purely numeric notation, and each DDC classification number ranges from three to n digits, and the longer the number, the more specific the category. As the word "decimal" suggests, the number ten plays a key role in the DDC; each new digit in a DDC number represent ten possible additional values.

DDC first order categories

0	Information, generalities [later added to this class: computer science]
1	Philosophy and psychology
2	Religion
3	Social sciences
4	Language
5	Science

(cont.)

DDC first order categories (cont.)

6	Technology
7	Arts and recreation
8	Literature
9	History and geography

Each of these ten categories of study is then broken down into ten sub-categories:

DDC second order for class 0: Information, generalities

00	Computer science, information, and general works
01	Bibliographies
02	Library and information sciences
03	Encyclopedias and books of facts
04	[Formerly Biographies]
05	Journals, magazine, and serials of general interest
06	Associations, organizations, and museums
07	News media, journalism, and publishing
08	Quotations
09	Manuscripts and rare books

Which are, likewise, further analyzed into ten sub-subcategories apiece:

DDC "hundreds": Information, generalities → Library and information sciences

020	Library and information sciences, general works
021	Library relationships
022	Administration of physical plant
023	Personnel management
024	[Unassigned]
025	Library operations

026	Libraries for specific subjects
027	General libraries
028	Reading and use of other information media
029	[Unassigned]

This iterative subdivision by tens does not end at the "one hundreds," but can be (theoretically) extended infinitely, with each new digit providing ten additional possibilities for subdivision. The resulting class number looks like a series of digits; a period (".") is typically placed between the third and fourth digit to help legibility.

There is much more, of course, to the DDC than just dividing by ten. Dewey provided, for example, patterns or sequences of classification that can be appended to existing Dewey numbers across the classification system. These "standard subdivisions" create a logical system of great depth and flexibility, enabling knowledgeable people to "read" and "write" Dewey numbers without recourse to the printed manuals. For the rest of us, the DDC provides useful tables and a "relative index" that maps from terms for concepts and fields of study back to specific Dewey Decimal classes. Much of this depth, however, is often unplumbed by the libraries that rely on DDC, as the classificatory power of the first three- or four-digit places is usually sufficient to provide a meaningful organizational structure. Regardless, however, of the level of specificity at which it is applied, DDC remains widely used throughout the world because it enables a flexible and user-friendly method of organizing resources.

LCC

The Library of Congress classification system is, as the name suggests, the system of classification that originated at the Library of Congress. Although it dates to around the same time as the DDC, the last quarter of the nineteenth century, LCC is in many ways the inverse of Dewey's classification system. Whereas DDC was the brainchild of an individual, the LCC comes out of the collaborative efforts of a generation of catalogers and classifiers at the Library of Congress. Where the DDC was intended, from its inception, to be a universal system that could be applied to any collection anywhere in the world, LCC began its life as—and remains to this day—the in-house classification system for the Library of Congress's own collection. (These collections are so vast in size and complete in scope that an "in-house" system is more than sufficient to accommodate collections of smaller size and ambition.) Where the DDC is a "synthetic" classification system, that is to say it enables classifiers to generate or synthesize new classification numbers according to the principle of division by tens, the LC is a wholly "enumerative" classification system.[14] This means, quite simply, that, for every discipline of study or domain of knowledge that can be classified according to LCC, there is a list (or "schedule") of available classification numbers, and the job of the classifier is primarily to determine where, in this prearranged order of topics, to assign a given document.

The primary LCC classes:

A   General Works

B   Philosophy, Psychology, and Religion

C   Auxiliary Sciences of History

D   General and Old World History

E   History of America

F   History of the United States and British, Dutch, French, and Latin America

G   Geography, Anthropology, and Recreation

H   Social Sciences

J   Political Science

K   Law

L   Education

M   Music

N   Fine Arts

P   Language and Literature

Q   Science

R   Medicine

S   Agriculture

T   Technology

U   Military Science

V   Naval Science

Z   Bibliography, Library Science, and
    General Information Resources

Unlike the DDC, LCC classification numbers feature a combination of letters and numbers. Letters account for the first two (or three, in some specific cases) elements of the classification number, indicating the top-level and broadest class, as well as the first level of subdivision. Note that under LCC, the top-level class serves as a home for general works within the discipline.

LCC Classes and subclasses: H (Social sciences)

H	Social sciences, general works
HA	Statistics
HB	Economic theory. Demography
HC	Economic history and conditions
HD	Industries. Land use. Labor
HE	Transportation and communications
HF	Commerce
HG	Finance
HJ	Public finance
HM	Sociology
HN	Social history and conditions. Social problems. Social reform
HQ	The Family. Marriage. Women
HS	Societies: Secret, benevolent, etc.
HT	Communities. Classes. Races
HV	Social pathology. Social and public welfare. Criminology
HX	Socialism. Communism. Utopias. Anarchism

After the class and subclass have been indicated by letters, LCC makes use of numbers to indicate specific topics within each subclass. Note that, unlike DDC, which treats all numbers as *decimals* (i.e., .1, .15, .2), class numbers under LCC are treated as *integers* (i.e., 1, 2 ... 15).

Extract from an LCC schedule: HM (Sociology)

HM425	Dictionaries. Encyclopedias
HM427	Terminology. Abbreviations. Notation
HM429	Directories
HM435	History of sociology. General works
HM437	History of sociology, by period: Ancient
HM439	History of sociology, by period: Medieval
HM441	History of sociology, by period: Modern to 1700
HM443	History of sociology, by period: 18th century
HM445	History of sociology, by period: 19th century
HM447	History of sociology, by period: 20th century. General works
HM449	History of sociology, by period: 20th century. Postmodernism
HM451	History of sociology, by period: 20th century. Post-industrial society

As this extract demonstrates, LCC, like the DDC, is also concerned with bringing concepts together into a hierarchical arrangement. For example, it brings works on the history of sociology and sociological thought together and groups them by period. It even further subdivides on period (twentieth century) into more specific categories. Where LCC differs from DDC, however, is that this hierarchical organization of the world is expressed in the printed schedules, but not in the classification numbers themselves. That is to say, for example, that the classification number HM435 refers to the general category of works on the history of sociology, whereas HM451 refers specifically to works on "the history of sociology in the twentieth century relating to post-industrial society," but the classification numbers themselves are of the same length; the DDC, following its own principles of subdivision by decimal digits, would yield a longer number for the more specific class.

Shelflisting is derived from the idea of "entering a resource into the shelf list." Many technical services departments maintain a single, staff-side index for every resource in the collection, arranged by call number, which is referred to as the "shelflist." Whereas classification proper is a practice meant to bring resources together with books on the same topic or in the same discipline, shelflisting is the process of adding a code that indicate a specific resource to that classification number. This final, unique address is called a "call number."

In many collections, shelflisting the name of the author or title is represented as a two- or three-letter abbreviation. In other places, the call number is completed through the use of an alphanumeric device known as a "cutter."[15] Derived from the author's name, or sometimes the resource's title, a cutter consists of one or two initial letters, followed by a number that is based on the remaining letters in the name or word. This provides both a unique alphanumeric element to add to a class number, but also works to keep resources under the same class number in alphabetical order by author or title. In most systems, the numeric portion of a cutter is treated as a decimal; this is key because it allows subsequent works to be inserted into the existing sequence and maintain an alphabetical arrangement.

Examples of Library of Congress cutters representing author surnames:

.**S73** Stark

.**S744** Stefani

.**S748** Stevens

.**S75** Sterling

.**S77** Strauss

MARC (Encoding Standard)

All resource descriptions begin with content standards, controlled vocabularies, and classification, but they must end by being encoded for machine reading. Ideally, catalogers could focus just on applying their complex content standards and controlled vocabularies to create high-quality resource descriptions, while encoding of those descriptions could happen behind the scenes in cataloging software clients. With BIBFRAME, cataloging practice will move in that direction. The end of Chapter 2 discusses the expected linked data environment which will use RDF triple statements to describe resources; and while it's helpful to have an understanding of the principles of linked data and some of its mechanics, the wonderful thing is that no one will need to be an expert coder or programmer to create triple statement descriptions.

For the present, however, catalogers must also be fluent in MARC. This encoding standard has indelibly shaped most catalogers' thinking about record creation because we enter descriptive data directly into MARC workforms, always making sure to use the right field tags and indicators and delimiter codes in each field.

As a result, catalogers have been pulling double duty for decades by not only creating good descriptive content, but also essentially hard-coding that content so it can be machine-actionable. You might think of it like writing a blog post but then also marking up that post with HTML code so it can be displayed online. In fact, it's helpful to think of learning MARC as learning a set of tags like HTML or CSS.

Again, you will need to devote time for a deep dive into MARC coding conventions, but let's look at the basics. MARC organizes information in a catalog record by using numbered fields (the numbers are sometimes referred to as field tags), each with two coded indicators and sometimes coded subfields within fields. The codes used to mark the beginning of a subfield are called delimiters. The following table shows some of the basic elements of a MARC record, though most records you view will be more complex.

Note the use of ISBD punctuation in some fields. For clarity, this example has some extra spaces and information, but usually the $a delimiter is assumed in cataloging work forms and therefore omitted from display, and spaces do not generally occur after delimiters. The purpose of indicators is usually to signal what type of information being recorded in that field; for instance, the second indicator 0 on the 650 field means that term used is drawn from the authorized LCSH thesaurus. A second indicator 4 would mean a local, uncontrolled term is being used instead.

FIELD TAG	INDICATORS	FIELD AND SUBFIELD CONTENTS
001	__	Control number
020	__	$a ISBN
040	__	$a Institution doing the cataloging (MARC organization code) $b Language of the catalog record (MARC language code) $c Institution submitting the record to OCLC $d Institution modifying the record
050	_4	$a Class number $b cutter & year
100	10	$a Lastname, Firstname, $d year of birth
245	10	$a Title : $b subtitle /$c statement of responsibility.
246	1_	$a Variant title
260 (AACR2 only)	__	$a Place of publication : $b publisher, $c year.
264 (RDA only)	_1	$a Place of publication : $b publisher, $c year.
300	__	$a Extent of resource : $b illustration information ; $c size.
500	__	$a Free text note about the manifestation (no item- or copy-specific notes)"
650	_0	$a Library of Congress Subject Heading $z Geographical Subdivision $v Form of resource.

Here is a true MARC record in action drawn from Michigan State University's online catalog:

```
001     44594071
003     OCoLC
005     20160530171649.0
008     000630r20001937nyu              000 1 eng
010     00058186
020     0060199490
035     44594071
040     DLC$cDLC$dYDX$dOCL$dEEM$dUtOrBLW
043     n-us---
049     EEMR
050 00  PS3515.U789$bT5 2000
050 00  PS3515.U789$bT5 2000
082 00  813/.52$221
100 1   Hurston, Zora Neale.
245 10  Their eyes were watching God /$cZora Neale
        Hurston ; with
        a foreword by Edwidge Danticat.
260     New York :$bHarperCollins,$c2000.
300     xxii, 231 pages ;$c22 cm
336     text$btxt$2rdacontent
337     unmediated$bn$2rdamedia
338     volume$bnc$2rdacarrier
650  0  African American women$vFiction.
655  7  Psychological fiction.$2lcgft
```

There are additional fields and information here that we don't have time to investigate but note that many public catalogs have a "MARC view" option on individual records which can be useful for new catalogers looking to pop the hood and see MARC at work.

When it was first developed in the early 1970s, MARC was an extraordinarily innovative approach to library automation. It permitted transmission of data between computers, which gave a huge boost to cooperative cataloging efforts and ultimately became the means by which library systems and databases could store, index, and display catalog records in online discovery interfaces.

But now, as can be imagined, this rigid set of numerical fields and subfields constrains the richness and discoverability of descriptive data. RDA implementation, for instance, was complicated by the inability of MARC to accommodate the kind of granular data RDA encourages us to record.

However, even when the cataloging community fully transitions to BIBFRAME, or whatever we ultimately choose as the next evolution of cataloging practice, a good knowledge of MARC will be essential for dealing with and transforming legacy data.

In addition, MARC provides a number of important code lists[16] for things like institutions, languages, countries, and more. These codes are intrinsic to cataloging practice and will likely continue to operate as useful controlled terms even after the MARC bibliographic and authority formats are retired.

OCLC offers some excellent free MARC tutorials, and their on-line *Bibliographic Formats and Standards* document is a go-to reference for every cataloger.[17] Colloquially referred to as *Bib Formats*, this site breaks down the technical usage and provides numerous examples for the use of every established MARC field, indicator, and subfield.

BEYOND CATALOGING

Creating one resource description after another certainly forms the bulk of a traditional cataloger's work, but there are many auxiliary functions you will be expected to understand and/or perform. The following tasks support, inform, and maintain the process of cataloging and the enormous amounts of descriptive data generated thereby.

Authority Work

Currently, authority records are created under the purview of RDA and MARC just like catalog records. Both these standards provide guidance for constructing and encoding access points for people, families, corporate bodies, conferences, and geographic places, as well as information that accompanies the authorized access point being established by the authority record.

Unlike bibliographic cataloging, however, catalogers must undergo specialized training to be eligible to contribute authority records to LC's National Authority File (NAF). The bodies and processes governing national authority work are covered in more detail in Chapter 2.

Authority records are also created for LC Subject Headings, Genre/Form Terms, and other vocabularies. Although catalogers can propose new terms for these vocabularies, authority record creation and maintenance is generally handled by the Library of Congress instead of catalogers at other institutions.

MARC authority records can be downloaded from OCLC and indexed in local library databases just like MARC bibliographic records, and though they do not display to the public, they provide some helpful background functionality in the public catalog. Generally, for instance, an author's name in a typical OPAC catalog record is hotlinked and clicking on that hotlink takes the user to other works by that same author. This collocation is accomplished by the presence of an authority record for that author in the library database, and the usage of that authority record's authorized access point in all associated bibliographic records.

As a new cataloger, you will need to be familiar with the look of authority records and the principles of their operation (see below for details about bibliographic file maintenance, for instance). As you perform copy or original cataloging, you will frequently need to search authority records in your bibliographic utility to see if an established form of name exists for an access point used in the record, or to confirm that the form of name used is actually for the correct entity.

Generally, it is not essential that you undergo training for authority record creation, at least not right off the bat. At larger institutions especially, there are some catalogers who specialize in authority work more than others, and their work is often sufficient for the whole institution. Catalogers at smaller institutions can participate in national authority work if they wish but can also choose to forgo this time-intensive responsibility and depend instead on cooperative cataloging to fill their authority needs.

Records in Your Library System

Typically, your catalog database will accommodate more than just bibliographic and authority records. Other "attached" records like order or purchase records may be kept there, as well as item records or holdings records to show patrons what exactly the library collection has and permit circulation of physical materials, check-in records that track the receipt of journal issues over time, and so forth. The types and operations of attached records differ somewhat in each proprietary library system, but their purpose is the same: facilitating inventory management.

Depending on the size of your institution, your cataloging work may involve creating, editing, or upkeep of such inventory management records. For instance, you may bring in a bibliographic record to copy catalog a DVD set, but then you might also need to create item records for each individual disc so that patrons can check out only the discs they need and not the entire set. You may in fact be responsible for not only cataloging and authority work, but all the processing that goes into preparing a resource for circulation— setting up the right loan rules, adding barcodes and call number labels, etc.

Most catalog database clients have functions that assist with processing like barcode scanning capabilities, label printers, and so on. Again, this is something your supervisor should be prepared to walk you through, but if you're learning on your own your library vendor will have trainings and tutorials available for understanding all the different types of inventory management functions you need to use.

Catalog Data Curation

With all of this bibliographic and authority and inventory data to manage, and after decades of changing standards and practice, you can imagine that a cataloger's job usually extends beyond working on new materials the library acquires.

There are dozens of factors that may require clean up or transformation of existing data. One common issue is bibliographic file maintenance (BFM), which is the adjustment work required when a new or updated authority record changes the access point that should be used in associated bibliographic records.

Libraries are notified of these changes to authority records through various channels, and some depend on added-on library system features or a vendor-provided service to keep up with BFM. But if you're at a small institution these tools may not be realistic, and the BFM work will need to be done manually.

Another common source of data clean-up is batch loading records into the library system. Batch loads can be tricky, and one small quirk could cause a slew of errors. Depending on your responsibilities, you might be on the hook for batch loading and for any resulting corrections required.

A major change in cataloging conventions could also render some of your older data obsolete. A good example is the retiring of the general material designation or GMD, a note about the format of the resource which was routinely included in the 245 field under AACR2, and which is now verboten under RDA. Many libraries decided to remove the GMD from thousands of their records after this change, and programmatically add the RDA content, media, and carrier fields instead.

If nothing else, you may realize you've been making a mistake in your cataloging for two weeks and you need to quickly fix all those records without anyone being the wiser. All catalogers have been there; don't let anyone tell you otherwise!

So once you become familiar with the structure and interaction of records in your local database, and the functions of each particular type of record, turn your attention to whatever reporting and batch editing tools are provided. These are the tools that permit powerful searches across all types of records and the editing of multiple records at once. You may only have to use these tools occasionally, but you will find them immensely helpful when the need arises. In the end, most catalogers find they must regularly handle some degree of database review, revision, and upkeep.

For this reason, you may also find it useful down the road to explore tools like MarcEdit and OpenRefine, which allow for even more powerful editing of batches of records than built-in database tools can usually provide. Some catalogers also learn regular expressions, a set of powerful text-matching commands, or programming languages like XSLT or Python, if their work involves a good deal of batch editing on a large scale. This is especially true of catalogers whose roles aren't as conventionally defined, and whose work involves creation and editing of all sorts of metadata.

Attempting such advanced techniques may seem intimidating at first but you will find once you master MARC and the principle operations of your database, programming languages and data transformation approaches will become more and more intuitive.

NOTES

1. A good starting point for further reading is Lois Mai Chan and Theodora Hogges, *Cataloging and classification: an introduction.* Lanham, Md.: Scarecrow Press, 2007.

2. The Library of Congress authorities file is available online at: http://authorities.loc.gov/. Interested readers may also wish to look at the Virtual International Authorities File, or VIAF, an experiment in aggregating the authorities information from a large number of countries, including the U.S.: https://viaf.org/.

3. American Library Association, Library Bill of Rights," 1939, revised through 1996, www.ala.org/advocacy/intfreedom/librarybill.

4. The work of Sanford Berman is widely regarded as the best starting point for a critical examination of subject cataloging in general, and the Library of Congress Subject Headings in particular. See, for further reading, his *Prejudices and antipathies: a tract on the LC subject heads concerning people* (Lanham, Md.: Scarecrow Press, 1971; reissued: Jefferson, N.C.: MacFarland & Co., 1993). Dr. Hope Olson's *The Power to Name* (Dordrecht, The Netherlands: Kluwer Academic Publishers, 2002) is another excellent examination of the ethical responsibilities of metadata creators and curators.

5. RDA Toolkit, http://access.rdatoolkit.org.

6. Association for Library Collections & Technical Services, Webinar Archive, www.ala.org/alcts/confevents/past/webinar.

7. Society of American Archivists, Describing Archives, A Content Standard, Second Edition (DACS), www2.archivists.org/standards/DACS.

8. Rare Books and Manuscripts Section, Descriptive Cataloging of Rare Materials, http://rbms.info/dcrm/.

9. Rare Books and Manuscripts Section, DCRM and RDA, http://rbms.info/dcrm/rda/.

10. Library of Congress, Classification Web, http://classificationweb.net.

11. Library of Congress, Library of Congress Subject Headings: Online Training, www.loc.gov/catworkshop/lcsh/.

12. OCLC, FAST (Faceted Application of Subject Terminology), www.oclc.org/research/themes/data-science/fast.html.

13. Library of Congress, Library of Congress Demographic Group Terms PDF Files, www.loc.gov/aba/publications/FreeLCDGT/freelcdgt.html.

14. Arlene G. Taylor, *Introduction to cataloging and classification.* 10th ed. (Westport, Conn.: Libraries Unlimited, 2006): p. 392–393.

15. Named after Charles A. Cutter who popularized their use.

16. Library of Congress, MARC Standards, www.loc.gov/marc.

17. OCLC, Bibliographic Formats and Standards, www.oclc.org/bibformats/en.html.

CHAPTER **FOUR**

Learning the Standards
Metadata

While "data about data" is catchy, that definition doesn't really help us understand what metadata is all about. In short, metadata is data about resources and is ubiquitous in our technology-driven world. These resources can include documents, books, images, collections, and more. Tagging images on Instagram, including title and artist information on Spotify, and creating descriptions on YouTube are all common ways people create metadata on a routine basis. Amazon's categories allow shoppers the ability to drill down and find the item they want quickly and efficiently. Metadata is not only a main driver of how these systems work, it also allows users to discover and share content with others.

Metadata creation in libraries, archives, and museums (LAMs) is an essential part of curating materials and objects. Early libraries held books inventories that have since transformed into card catalogs and now Online Public Access Catalogs (OPACS). Anne J. Gilliland defines metadata as "the value-added information [librarians] create to arrange, describe, track, and otherwise enhance access to information objects and the physical items and collections related to those objects."[1] In order to accomplish this librarians work with different types of metadata that capture this varied information and work with metadata standards within these types that allow for consistent and clear description.

Most metadata used in LAMs describe resources. However, you may also find marked-up documents. The Text Encoding Initiative (TEI) is the most commonly used text markup seen in LAMs. With this type of encoding a text document (such as a poem) is marked up for analysis. For more information, see the Text Encoding Initiative website.[2]

SAMPLE TEI TAGS FOR A VERSE[3]

```
<sp>
 <speaker>First Voice</speaker>
 <lg type="stanza" part="I">
  <l>But why drives on that ship so fast</l>
  <l>Withouten wave or wind?</l>
 </lg>
</sp>
<sp>
 <speaker>Second Voice</speaker>
 <lg type="stanza" part="F">
  <l>The air is cut away before,</l>
  <l>And closes from behind.</l>
 </lg>
</sp>
```

TYPES OF METADATA

Metadata work requires knowledge of at least a few descriptive, value, content, and encoding standards. Those outlined here are by no means a comprehensive list, but rather, a sampling of the most commonly used standards in libraries, archives, and museums. Additional information on different types of metadata standards can be found in Chapter 6.

The three main types of metadata seen in LAMs are Descriptive, Structural, and Administrative metadata. Most descriptive metadata standards interweave components of each type of metadata to form a comprehensive metadata record (e.g., MARC 21, MODS, and Dublin Core, the latter two discussed below). Although you will most likely encounter these different types of metadata together in one record, it's worthwhile to explore the different types individually.

Descriptive Metadata

Descriptive metadata is the type librarians are most familiar with. Descriptive metadata provides information about the item being described, such as a title, date information, and an abstract. This information is key for resource discovery.

Data Structure Standards

Data structure standards dictate the element set used to describe resources. Data structure standards provide the "containers" for descriptive information. These standards tell you the minimal fields required to describe an item according to the standard. The most familiar data structure standard in libraries is MARC21, but for digital repositories MODS and Dublin Core are commonly used.

Dublin Core

Dublin Core (DC) is a very popular metadata standard because of its inherent flexibility and minimal training required for implementation. The Dublin on the name comes from Dublin, Ohio, the headquarters of OCLC. With only fifteen core fields, it's an easy standard to apply in digital repositories. It's a particularly popular standard for cultural heritage institutions that do not have a staff trained in traditional library cataloging. Each DC element is repeatable and optional. Additionally, there are no rules for how the elements are ordered.

Simple Dublin Core Fields

- Title
- Creator
- Subject
- Description
- Publisher
- Contributor
- Date
- Type
- Format
- Identifier
- Source
- Language
- Relation
- Coverage
- Rights

There are some major drawbacks to DC, particularly its inherent flexibility. For instance, there are no cataloging rules commonly associated with Dublin Core (e.g., like RDA for MARC and MODS), so even though all the dates are in the "date" field, there can be various iterations that makes interpreting the data difficult. For instance, one record could use the format "1959 June 1," while another uses "June 1, 1959" and both are valid. Additionally, because of this variance, computers aren't able to read the data, making search and discovery more difficult.

Because there are only fifteen core elements, transforming data in and out of more robust metadata standards can get tricky. For example, the MODS fields for abstract, note, and table of contents all map to the DC description field. Once in a DC description field, they lose the context of whether the data is an abstract, note, or table of contents. Converting DC to MODS defaults to a note field.

SAMPLE DUBLIN CORE RECORD

```
<oai_dc:dc xmlns:dc="http://purl.org/dc/elements/1.1/"
xmlns:oai_dc="http://www.openarchives.org/OAI/2.0/oai_
dc/" xmlns:xsi="http://www.w3.org/2001/XMLSchema-inst
ance"xsi:schemaLocation="http://www.openarchives.org/
OAI/2.0/oai_dc/ http://www.openarchives.org/OAI/2.0/
oai_dc.xsd">
  <dc:title>
   Northwest Turfgrass Topics. Vol. 1 no. 1 (1959
   February)
  </dc:title>
  <dc:subject>Lawns--Periodicals</dc:subject>
  <dc:subject>Grasses--Periodicals</dc:subject>
  <dc:publisher>Northwest Turfgrass Association</
   dc:publisher>
  <dc:date>1959-02</dc:date>
  <dc:type>Text</dc:type>
  <dc:type>Periodicals</dc:type>
  <dc:format>4 pages</dc:format>
  <dc:identifier>nwtgt:1</dc:identifier>
  <dc:identifier>1959feb</dc:identifier>
  <dc:language>English</dc:language>
  <dc:relation>Northwest turfgrass topics</dc:relation>
  <dc:rights>In Copyright</dc:rights>
</oai_dc:dc>
```

Qualified Dublin Core furthers the fifteen element set to include three more elements: Audience, RightsHolder, and Provenance. Qualified Dublin Core also allows further information on terms and formatting within the XML tags using "xsitype."

SAMPLE QUALIFIED DUBLIN CORE RECORD

```
<oai_dc:dc xmlns:dc="http://purl.org/dc/elements/1.1/"
xmlns:oai_dc="http://www.openarchives.org/OAI/2.0/
oai_dc/" xmlns:xsi="http://www.w3.org/2001/XMLSchema-
instance" xsi:schemaLocation="http://www.openarchives.
org/OAI/2.0/oai_dc/ http://www.openarchives.org/OAI/2.0/
oai_dc.xsd">
<dc:title>
Northwest Turfgrass Topics. Vol. 1 no. 1 (1959 February)
</dc:title>
<dc:subject xsitype="LCSH">Lawns--Periodicals</
dc:subject>
<dc:subject xsitype="LCSH">Grasses--Periodicals</
dc:subject>
<dc:publisher>Northwest Turfgrass Association</
dc:publisher>
<dc:date xsitype="W3CDTF">1959-02</dc:date>
<dc:type xsitype="DCMIType">Text</dc:type>
<dc:type>Periodicals</dc:type>
<dc:format>4 pages</dc:format>
<dc:identifier>nwtgt:1</dc:identifier>
<dc:identifier>1959feb</dc:identifier>
<dc:language >English</dc:language>
<dc:relation>Northwest turfgrass topics</dc:relation>
<dc:rights>In Copyright</dc:rights>
</oai_dc:dc>
```

MODS

Based on the MARC standard, MODS is sometimes described as "Marc lite." Short for Metadata Object Description Standard, MODS is governed by the Library of Congress and is a shorter, human-readable standard based on the MARC format. MODS is far more robust than Dublin Core, and allows for much more granularity and instructions for describing material.

MODS is very popular in libraries for many reasons. Because its history is tied to MARC, crosswalking metadata from MARC to MODS keeps a lot of the context. This is particularly important because libraries have a lot of MARC data! Additionally, the human-readable language tags are far more user friendly than the MARC tag numbers. MODS also condenses the data repeated in a MARC record into fewer fields for more clear and concise descriptions. The hierarchy within the MODS standard continues to allow robust descriptions since context can be inferred through parent tags. The MODS website[4] also provides guidance on using the MODS standard with examples.

MODS Top Level Elements

- titleInfo
- Name
- typeOfResource
- Genre
- originInfo
- Language
- physicalDescription
- Abstract
- tableOfContents
- targetAudience
- note
- subject
- classification
- relatedItem
- identifier
- location
- accessCondition
- part
- extension
- recordInfo

SAMPLE MODS RECORD

```
<mods:mods>
<mods:titleInfo>
<mods:title>Northwest turfgrass topics</mods:title>
<mods:partNumber>Vol. 1 no. 1 (1959 February)</
mods:partNumber>
</mods:titleInfo>
<mods:name>
<mods:namePart>Northwest Turfgrass Association</
mods:namePart>
<mods:role>
<mods:roleTerm>publisher</mods:roleTerm>
```

```
</mods:role>
<mods:role>
<mods:roleTerm>copyright holder</mods:roleTerm>
</mods:role>
</mods:name>
<mods:typeOfResource>text</mods:typeOfResource>
<mods:genre authority>Text</mods:genre>
<mods:genre>Periodicals</mods:genre>
<mods:genre >text</mods:genre>
<mods:place>
<mods:placeTerm>Puyallup, Washington</mods:placeTerm>
</mods:place>
<mods:publisher>Northwest Turfgrass Association</
mods:publisher>
<mods:dateIssued>1959-02</mods:dateIssued>
<mods:issuance>serial</mods:issuance>
<mods:frequency>Three times a year</mods:frequency>
</mods:originInfo>
<mods:language>
<mods:languageTerm>English</mods:languageTerm>
</mods:language>
<mods:physicalDescription>
<mods:form>print</mods:form>
<mods:form>unmediated</mods:form>
<mods:form>volume</mods:form>
<mods:extent>4 pages</mods:extent>
<mods:digitalOrigin>reformatted digital</
mods:digitalOrigin>
</mods:physicalDescription>
<mods:accessCondition>In Copyright</
mods:accessCondition>
<mods:subject authority="lcsh" authorityURI="http://
id.loc.gov/authorities/subjects">
<mods:topic>Lawns</mods:topic>
<mods:genre>Periodicals</mods:genre>
</mods:subject>
<mods:subject authority="lcsh" authorityURI="http://
id.loc.gov/authorities/subjects">
<mods:topic>Grasses</mods:topic>
<mods:genre>Periodicals</mods:genre>
</mods:subject>
```

(cont.)

```
<mods:classification authority="lcc">SB433.A1 N6 v.1 no.1
1959</mods:classification>
<mods:relatedItem type="host">
<mods:titleInfo>
<mods:title>Northwest Turfgrass Topics</mods:title>
</mods:titleInfo>
<mods:identifier type="local">(OCoLC)11627018</
mods:identifier>
<mods:recordInfo>
<mods:descriptionStandard>aacr</
mods:descriptionStandard>
<mods:recordContentSource>Michigan State University.
Libraries</mods:recordContentSource>
<mods:recordCreationDate\>2018-01-10</
mods:recordCreationDate>
<mods:recordIdentifier>nwtgt:1959feb</
mods:recordIdentifier>
<mods:languageOfCataloging>
<mods:languageTerm>eng</mods:languageTerm>
</mods:languageOfCataloging>
</mods:recordInfo>
</mods:mods>
```

Schema.org

Schema.org was launched in 2011 by large search engine companies to create a vocabulary for structured data markup in web pages. The vocabulary is based on an RDF vocabulary and can be coded into websites to promote search engine optimization. As of 2016, Schema.org claimed to be used in over ten million websites!

Schema.org defines about 600 types and over 800 properties. Types are defined as RDF classes and include things like creative work, book, map, or photograph. Within these types are certain properties you can describe. In the example below, creativeWork is the type, and the properties are: author, contentRating, image, and name.

SAMPLE J-SON LD MARKUP FROM SCHEMA.ORG WEBSITE

```
<script type="application/ld+json">
{
  "@context": "http://schema.org",
  "@type": "CreativeWork",
  "author": "Sony",
  "contentRating": "Mature",
  "image": "videogame.jpg",
  "name": "Resistance 3: Fall of Man"
}
</script>
```

Libraries are experimenting with Schema.org in an attempt to enhance discoverability of their resources. As of 2017, results are inconclusive. This is in part because the large search engine companies are not sharing how they use the markup in their search algorithms. Although Schema.org has various object types for cultural objects in their creative work vocabulary, the optimization seems to be focused on items labeled as "products." OCLC has undertaken a project to embed Schema.org vocabulary into Worldcat as part of their push towards Linked Data.

SAMPLE SCHEMA.ORG RECORD

```
<http://www.worldcat.org/oclc/981121049> # The secret
garden
    a schema:Book, bgn:SoundRecording, schema:
    CreativeWork, schema:AudioObject ; library:oclcnum
    "981121049" ; library:placeOf Publication <http://
    id.loc.gov/vocabulary/countries/enk> ;
    rdfs:comment "Unknown 'gen' value: snd" ;
    schema:about <http://experiment.worldcat.org/entity/
    work/data/14482763#Topic/gardens> ; #
Gardens
    schema:about <http://experiment.worldcat.org/entity/
    work/data/ 14482763#Place/england_yorkshire> ; #
    England--Yorkshire.
```

(cont.)

SAMPLE SCHEMA.ORG RECORD (cont.)

```
   schema:about <http://experiment.worldcat.org/entity/
   work/data/14482763#Topic/people_with_disabilities> ;
   # People with disabilities
   schema:about <http://experiment.worldcat.org/entity/
work/data/14482763#Topic/orphans> ; # Orphans
   schema:about <http://experiment.worldcat.org/
entity/work/data/14482763#Place/yorkshire_england> ; #
Yorkshire (England)
   schema:audience <http://www.worldcat.org/title/-/
oclc/981121049#Audience> ;
   schema:author <http://experiment.worldcat.org/
entity/work/data/14482763#Person/burnett_frances_
hodgson_1849_1924> ; # Frances Hodgson Burnett
   schema:bookEdition "Unabridged." ;
   schema:bookFormat bgn:AudioBook ;
   schema:contributor <http://experiment.worldcat.org/
entity/work/data/14482763#Person/reid_beryl_1920_1996> ;
# Beryl Reid
   schema:contributor <http://experiment.worldcat.org/
entity/work/data/14482763#Person/walter_harriet> ; #
Harriet Walter
   schema:datePublished "2017" ;
   schema:description "Harriet Walter and Beryl Reid
star in this full-cast adaptation of the much-loved
children's classic. When spoilt young orphan Mary Lennox
is brought back from India to live in her uncle's house
on the Yorkshire Moors, she finds the blunt ways of the
staff at Misselthwaite Manor an unpleasant shock. Bored
and miserable, it seems as though life in England will
be awful. But Misselthwaite has hidden delights and,
when Mary begins to discover them, nothing is the same
again. First, there is the secret garden - and with it
comes a boy who knows all the wonders of the country. He
can even talk to the birds! Then, as the old house gives
up its biggest secret, Mary forms a magical friendship.
Frances Hodgson Burnett's charming story is played out
with all the freshness and warmth of the original novel
in this BBC Radio full-cast dramatization."@en ;
   schema:exampleOfWork <http://worldcat.org/entity/
work/id/14482763> ;
```

```
    schema:genre "Children's audiobooks"@en ;
    schema:genre "Audiobooks"@en ;
    schema:genre "Juvenile works"@en ;
    schema:genre "Downloadable audio books"@en ;
    schema:genre "Fiction"@en ;
    schema:inLanguage "en" ;
    schema:isPartOf <http://experiment.worldcat.org/
entity/work/data/14482763#Series/bbc_children_s_
classics> ; # BBC children's classics.
    schema:name "The secret garden"@en ;
    schema:productID "981121049" ;
    schema:url <https://samples.overdrive.
com/?crid=2fbc164c-ef06-45ac-b786-d84e47c17acf&.epub-
sample.overdrive.com> ;
    schema:url <https://www.overdrive.com/
search?q=2FBC164C-EF06-45AC-B786-D84E47C17ACF> ;
    schema:url <https://excerpts.cdn.overdrive.com/
FormatType-425/0211-1/3151731-TheSecretGarden.mp3> ;
    schema:workExample <http://worldcat.org/
isbn/9781785298318> ;
    wdrs:describedby <http://www.worldcat.org/title/-/
oclc/981121049> ;
```

Data Value Standards (i.e., Controlled Vocabularies)

Data value standards are the controlled vocabulary terms that go into the structured containers. Controlled vocabularies are a vital part of metadata creation to aid in search and retrieval of information. Controlled vocabularies are typically used for names, subjects, and genre/form terms.

Like cataloging librarians, metadata librarians need working knowledge of Library of Congress vocabularies, such as Library of Congress Subject Headings (LCSH), Name Authority File (NAF), and Genre/Form Terms (LCGFT). Although these value standards are usually enough for cataloging, metadata librarians typically need familiarity with a few additional vocabularies such as Getty's Art & Architecture Thesaurus and Thesaurus of Geographic Names, Dublin Core Metadata Initiative Type Vocabulary (DCMI Type), and MODS Type of Resource Vocabulary.

Data Content Standards

Content standards dictate how metadata should be formatted. This ensures consistency, which in turn allows for the data to be read by machines and reused in other systems (for example, the ILS, ArchivesSpace, or a digital repository). By using a content standard, computers are better able to predict the format of the data, and thus programming languages can manipulate the data for different needs.

Content standards are commonly undervalued since they require a steep learning curve and are heavy in documentation. But to avoid problems going forward, it's immensely important to choose a content standard that best suits your needs.

When learning metadata content standards, experience and exposure to cataloging is immensely helpful The two most common content standards in LAMs are AACR2 and RDA (for more information on these two, see Chapter 3). Other common content standards in LAMs are Describing Archives: A Content Standard (DACS), Cataloging Cultural Objects (CCO), the International Standard for Bibliographic Description (ISBD), or Descriptive Cataloging of Rare Materials (DCRM). Depending on the type of material you are describing, one content standard will usually work better than others, and you always have the option to create a hybrid record.

Content standards are tricky because they usually have inherited biases based on their origin community. For instance, RDA is great at providing guidelines for books and other printed material, but falls short for describing archival material. DACS is best for describing archival collections, but DCRM(G) does a better job at describing individual photographs in a digital repository.

Structural Metadata

Structural metadata indicates the structure of the item being described, such as book chapters or articles within a larger book. This is commonly seen in HTML, with heading tags showing hierarchy and structure within the document. Structural metadata is also a part of PREMIS (described below) for recording information about the structure of a digital object.

```
<html xmlns="http://www.w3.org/1999/xhtml">
    <head>
        <title>Sample HTML</title>
    </head>
    <body>
        <h1>Heading 1</h1>
        <p>Paragraph 1</p>
        <p>Paragraph 2</p>
        <h1>Heading 2</h1>
        <p>Paragraph</p>
    </body>
</html>
```

Administrative Metadata

Administrative metadata provides information that helps curate and manage a resource, such as file type information, when and by whom the digital object was created, and information on how the resourced can be accessed. The three main types of administrative metadata are rights management metadata, technical metadata, and preservation metadata.

Rights Management Metadata

Rights management metadata encompases intellectual property information. Two pillars of rights metadata describe how a resource can be used and who can use the resource. Material may have restrictions on reuse, such as prohibiting cropping or adjusting color. Others may require a credit statement crediting the photographer, donor, or institution where the material is housed. Additionally, sensitive material or material under copyright may be restricted to use within a repository (physically or digitally).

Copyright status is a key part of rights management metadata. Copyright can be quite confusing when dealing with cultural heritage objects. Rightsstatements.org is a popular resource for crafting rights statements for cultural heritage institutions. The site provides a set of standardized statements ranging from material being completely unavailable to completely open and is used by large aggregators such as the Digital Public Library of America and

Europeana. Creative Commons is a useful and popular site. It provides six licences with varying levels of permissions for creative works. Unlike Rightsstatements.org, Creative Commons are a bit more vague and not specifically intended for cultural heritage collections.

Technical Metadata

Technical metadata includes information on how the resource can be viewed and details about how it was created. Examples include the scanning resolution on an image and the date the digital object was created. Metadata for Images in XML Schema (MIX) is a technical metadata standard administered by NISO and the Library of Congress.

Preservation Metadata

Preservation metadata provides information to help in preserving the item, such as information on a past conservation treatment the item received. The five components of preservation metadata are:

> **Provenance:** What is the ownership history of this resource?
>
> **Authenticity:** Is the digital object what it purports to be?
>
> **Preservation activity:** What has been done to preserve it?
>
> **Technical environment:** What is needed to render and use it?
>
> **Rights management:** What intellectual restrictions and rules must be observed in preservation actions?

PREservation Metadata:
Implementation Strategies (PREMIS)

PREMIS is a preservation metadata standard that provides information necessary in digital preservation, tracks preservation actions on a resource, and records information about the actor responsible for the action. Keeping metadata on preservation efforts is important as libraries acquire more and more digital content that needs to be available indefinitely. In 2005, the Library of Congress released the PREMIS Data Dictionary Report, which included the report, a dictionary of elements for digital preservation, a glossary, and usage examples. PREMIS is managed at the Library of Congress by an editorial board, and version 3.0 was released in June 2015.

PREMIS defines five entities that are described or acted upon in digital preservation systems:

- Objects: information units upon which preservation actions are taken. These include:
  - Intellectual entities
  - Representations
  - Files
  - Bitstreams
- Environments: hardware or software in which content resides
- Events: actions taken for digital preservation
- Agents: names of people, organizations, or software
- Rights: assert permission information over content

Digital repository systems such as Fedora and DSpace generate PREMIS metadata when actions are taken within the repository. If you are using a digital repository, be sure to check if the system is recording this metadata and that is is being recorded accurately.

ENCODING STANDARDS

XML

XML stands for eXtensible Markup Language and is a World Wide Web Consortium (W3) standard for encoding data. The main premise of XML is to mark up data while keeping everything human-readable. XML markup describes the structure of the data; XSL (detailed below) transforms the data into a presentable format (such as HTML or PDF).

XML documents are usually associated with a schema that sets the validation rules for that particular XML. MODS, MARCXML, and Dublin Core are metadata standards that have an associated schema to ensure that the elements required in the standard are in the document and formatted correctly.

XML Namespaces

XML namespaces provide a way to declare which standard you are using to describe your data. The standard dictates which elements and attributes are allowed in the document and is declared using the Uniform Resource Identifier (URI) for the standard. They also allow you to differentiate element names if you are using different descriptive standards that use the same element name.

The syntax for declaring a namespace uses a reserved XML attribute "xmlns." Elements are then bound implicitly (without a prefix) or explicitly (with a prefix) to a particular namespace. If elements are explicitly bound, every element in that dataset will have the prefix declared in the namespace part of the document.

In the following example, the yellow highlighted section is the namespace declaration that links to the purl.org namespace for Dublin Core. If you follow the URL, you find an XML document describing the elements and attributes found in Dublin Core. It's important to note that namespaces are not required to be locations (i.e, URLs). Namespaces are names—they are conceptual placeholders and do not have to resolve to anything. Additionally, you can put a namespace in any element within your document, but it's best practice to declare namespaces at the top for clarity. It's also best practice to have a resolvable URL for namespaces so users can learn more about the standards used in the description.

```
<oai_dc:dc xmlns:dc="http://purl.org/dc/elements/1.1/"
xmlns:oai_dc="http://www.openarchives.org/OAI/2.0/
oai_dc/" xmlns:xsi="http://www.w3.org/2001/XMLSchema-
instance" xsi:schemaLocation="http://www.openarchives.
org/OAI/2.0/oai_dc/ http://www.openarchives.org/OAI/2.0/
oai_dc.xsd">
    <dc:title>Northwest Turfgrass Topics</dc:title>
    <dc:subject>Lawns--Periodicals</dc:subject>
    <dc:subject>Grasses--Periodicals</dc:subject>
    <dc:description>This archive, an ongoing cooperative
project of the Northwest Turfgrass Association and the
Michigan State University Libraries, features public
access to Northwest Turfgrass Topics from 1959-1997. For
questions or comments about this archive or the search
```

```
engine, contact the Turfgrass Information Center. </
dc:description>
    <dc:publisher>Sisters, Oregon : Turfgrass
Connections</dc:publisher>
    <dc:date>1959/1997</dc:date>
    <dc:type>text</dc:type>
    <dc:type>periodicals</dc:type>
    <dc:format>application/pdf</dc:format>
    <dc:identifier>nwtgt:root</dc:identifier>
    <dc:identifier>(OCoLC)11627018</dc:identifier>
    <dc:language>eng</dc:language>
</oai_dc:dc>
```

XML Structure

XML is structured using tags to form an element. The element consists of an opening tag, some text, and then a closing tag that uses a "/" to close the element. Although it's not required, tags in XML are usually written in all lower case. However, XML is case sensitive, and case must stay consistent.

VALID	NOT VALID
`<tag>TEXT</tag>`	`<tag>TEXT</TAG>`

Tags can become more complicated by including attributes. Attributes are useful when adding additional information beyond the text surrounded by the tags. Attribute values must be written within quotation marks.

```
<tag attribute-name="attribute-value">CONTENT</tag>
```

In addition, attributes and elements must not contain whitespace, or punctuation other than hyphen, period, or underscore. They may contain letters, numbers, or ideographs, but they must begin with a letter or underscore.

VALID	NOT VALID
`<title>`	`<1title>`
`<publication_information>`	`<publication information>`
`<autho100r>`	`<100author>`

Well-formed XML must have a closing tag.

```
<element-tag attribute-name="attribute-value">CONTENT</
element-tag>
```

Some XML elements are formatted so only one tag is present with the closing "/" added at the end of the tag. Because it includes the "/" the tag is considered closed and thus, valid.

```
<element-tag attribute-name="attribute-value" />
```

XML has a hierarchical tree structure. Elements nest within each other to create a valid XML document. A Russian nesting doll is a metaphor for how the tags are structured. You need to close the inner ones first before closing the next layer and so on.

VALID	NOT VALID
<person><name>John</name></person>	<person><name>John</person></name>

The top most level in an XML document is called the root. All valid XML documents require a root that subsequent tags are enclosed within. All tags are nested within each other.

```
SAMPLE DUBLIN CORE XML RECORD

<?xml version="1.0" encoding="UTF-8"?>
<oai_dc:dc xmlns:dc="http://purl.org/dc/elements/1.1/"
xmlns:oai_dc="http://www.openarchives.org/OAI/2.0/
oai_dc/" xmlns:xsi="http://www.w3.org/2001/XMLSchema-
instance" xsi:schemaLocation="http://www.openarchives.
org/OAI/2.0/oai_dc/ http://www.openarchives.org/OAI/2.0/
oai_dc.xsd">
    <dc:title>Northwest Turfgrass Topics</dc:title>
    <dc:subject>Lawns--Periodicals</dc:subject>
    <dc:subject>Grasses--Periodicals</dc:subject>
    <dc:description>This archive, an ongoing cooperative
project of the Northwest Turfgrass Association and the
```

```
Michigan State University Libraries, features public
access to Northwest Turfgrass Topics from 1959-1997.</
dc:description>
    <dc:publisher>Sisters, Oregon : Turfgrass
Connections</dc:publisher>
    <dc:date>1959/1997</dc:date>
    <dc:type>text</dc:type>
    <dc:type>periodicals</dc:type>
    <dc:format>application/pdf</dc:format>
    <dc:identifier>nwtgt:root</dc:identifier>
    <dc:identifier>(OCoLC)11627018</dc:identifier>
    <dc:language>eng</dc:language>
</oai_dc:dc>
```

XML Schemas

XML defines the structure of an XML document. As stated on the W3schools XML Schema tutorial, XML schemas define and enforce rules for:

- the elements and attributes that can appear in a document
- the number of (and order of) child elements
- data types for elements and attributes
- default and fixed values for elements and attributes

Metadata standards written in XML have a schema available online. Both MODS and DC have schemas available from the Library of Congress and DCMI, respectively. Once you associate the appropriate schema to your document, you can validate your document against the schema to ensure your document is standard compliant. Text editing programs such as Oxygen have user-friendly ways to associate your XML document with an XML schema so you can ensure your data is valid as you work.

MODS SCHEMA EXAMPLE

```
*********************************************************
*    Top Level Element <titleInfo>                      *
*********************************************************


-->
<xs:element name="titleInfo" type="titleInfoDefinition"/>
<!--    -->
  <xs:complexType name="titleInfoDefinition">
    <xs:choice minOccurs="0" maxOccurs="unbounded">
    <xs:element ref="title"/>
    <xs:element ref="subTitle"/>
    <xs:element ref="partNumber"/>
    <xs:element ref="partName"/>
    <xs:element ref="nonSort"/>
  </xs:choice>
  <xs:attribute name="type">
    <xs:simpleType>
      <xs:restriction base="xs:string">
        <xs:enumeration value="abbreviated"/>
        <xs:enumeration value="translated"/>
        <xs:enumeration value="alternative"/>
        <xs:enumeration value="uniform"/>
      </xs:restriction>
    </xs:simpleType>
  </xs:attribute>
  <xs:attribute name="otherType"/>
  <xs:attribute name="supplied" fixed="yes"/>
  <xs:attribute name="altRepGroup" type="xs:string"/>
  <xs:attributeGroup ref="altFormatAttributeGroup"/>
  <xs:attribute name="nameTitleGroup" type="xs:string"/>
  <xs:attribute name="usage" fixed="primary"/>
  <xs:attribute name="ID" type="xs:ID"/>
  <xs:attributeGroup ref="authorityAttributeGroup"/>
  <xs:attributeGroup ref="xlink:simpleLink"/>
  <xs:attributeGroup ref="languageAttributeGroup"/>
  <xs:attribute name="displayLabel" type="xs:string"/>
</xs:complexType>
<!--
```

```
********    Subordinate Elements for <titleInfo>
  -->
<xs:element name="title" type="stringPlusLanguage"/>
<xs:element name="subTitle" type="stringPlusLanguage"/>
<xs:element name="partNumber"
type="stringPlusLanguage"/>
<xs:element name="partName" type="stringPlusLanguage"/>
<!--

*********  nonSort definition revised in 3.6. to add
attribute xml:space.

-->
<xs:element name="nonSort">
  <xs:complexType>
    <xs:simpleContent>
      <xs:extension base="stringPlusLanguage">
        <xs:attribute ref="xml:space"/>
      </xs:extension>
    </xs:simpleContent>
  </xs:complexType>
</xs:element>
<!--
```

JavaScript Object Notation for Linked Data (JSON-LD)

JSON-LD is a light-weight, easy-to-use format for encoding linked data in JSON. It's commonly used to store metadata, particularly in websites. More information on JSON-LD can be found on the JSON-LD website.[5]

The standard uses curly brackets and "@" to denote different elements. JSON-LD is commonly paired with Schema.org vocabularies to assist in search engine optimization. Typically, libraries still prefer XML to store metadata, but JSON-LD is a promising and ever-more popular standard for storing and displaying metadata.

SAMPLE FROM JSON-LD WEBSITE USING DUBLIN CORE

```json
{
  "@context": {
    "dc": "http://purl.org/dc/elements/1.1/",
    "ex": "http://example.org/vocab#",
    "xsd": "http://www.w3.org/2001/XMLSchema#",
    "ex:contains": {
      "@type": "@id"
    }
  },
  "@graph": [
    {
      "@id": "http://example.org/library",
      "@type": "ex:Library",
      "ex:contains": "http://example.org/library/the-republic"
    },
    {
      "@id": "http://example.org/library/the-republic",
      "@type": "ex:Book",
      "dc:creator": "Plato",
      "dc:title": "The Republic",
      "ex:contains": "http://example.org/library/the-republic#introduction"
    },
    {
      "@id": "http://example.org/library/the-republic#introduction",
      "@type": "ex:Chapter",
      "dc:description": "An introductory chapter on The Republic.",
      "dc:title": "The Introduction"
    }
  ]
}
```

PROGRAMMING LANGUAGES

Metadata that adheres to standards gives librarians great flexibility to manipulate, transform, and repurpose that data. Thus, some knowledge of programming languages will give the new CML a leg-up in their daily work.

XSLT

XSL (eXtensible Stylesheet Language) is a styling language for XML. XSLT stands for XSL Transformations. XSLT is used to transform XML documents into stylized, presentation formats, such as HTML or PDF. In metadata work, XSLT is mostly used to transform XML metadata from one standard to another.

XSLT can be written using version 1.0, 2.0, or 3.0. Version 3.0 was released in June 2017 so, as of this writing, most XSLTs available are in version 1.0 or 2.0. Some of the major differences between 1.0 and 2.0 are that 2.0 can group data better, use regular expressions for manipulating text strings, and allows for the creation of unique functions. The version of XSLT will be declared at the top of the document. Knowing which version of XSLT is being used is important when selecting the processor that will transform the data. Older processors can only handle version 1.0.

If you are working with a standard metadata schema, numerous XSLTs are freely available online. The Library of Congress hosts many XSLT documents for transforming metadata across standards. For instance, on the MODS documentation site, you can download XSLTs to transform MODS into Dublin Core, MARCXML, or HTML. Many metadata librarians happily share their code on sites such as GitHub. Additionally, the free software MarcEdit has a number of XSLTs including in the free download. Because these are generic XSLTs, they may require some editing to finesse the results, such as creating regular expressions to add or remove punctuation.

The W3 school has an excellent introduction to XSLT available on their website (www.w3schools.com/xml/xsl_intro.asp). For library specific training and examples, XSLT workshops and webinars are routinely held through library professional organizations such as the Association for Library Collections & Technical Services (ALCTS), the Library and Information Technology Association (LITA), Online Audiovisual Catalogers, Inc. (OLAC), Code4Lib, the Association of

College & Research Libraries (ACRL), or the Association of Research Libraries (ARL). These workshops vary greatly on the level of detail included in the presentation, but are a great way to learn XSLT for practical library uses.

XSL documents are written in XML. Below is a snippet of the MODS to DC stylesheet freely available on the Library of Congress MODS website. As you can see, there are elements that allow for decisions such as the "if" clauses to determine which dc:type to use in transforming the mods:typeOfResource to dc:type.

```
<xsl:template match="mods:typeOfResource">
<xsl:if test="@collection='yes'">
<dc:type>Collection</dc:type>
</xsl:if>
<xsl:if test=". ='software' and ../
mods:genre='database'">
<dc:type>Dataset</dc:type>
</xsl:if>
<xsl:if test=".='software' and ../mods:genre='online
system or service'">
<dc:type>Service</dc:type>
</xsl:if>
<xsl:if test=".='software'">
<dc:type>Software</dc:type>
</xsl:if>
<xsl:if test=".='cartographic material'">
<dc:type>Image</dc:type>
</xsl:if>
<xsl:if test=".='multimedia'">
<dc:type>InteractiveResource</dc:type>
</xsl:if>
<xsl:if test=".='moving image'">
<dc:type>MovingImage</dc:type>
</xsl:if>
<xsl:if test=".='three dimensional object'">
<dc:type>PhysicalObject</dc:type>
</xsl:if>
<xsl:if test="starts-with(.,'sound recording')">
<dc:type>Sound</dc:type>
</xsl:if>
```

```
<xsl:if test=".='still image'">
<dc:type>StillImage</dc:type>
</xsl:if>
<xsl:if test=". ='text'">
<dc:type>Text</dc:type>
</xsl:if>
<xsl:if test=".='notated music'">
<dc:type>Text</dc:type>
</xsl:if>
</xsl:template>
```

Python

Python is a (relatively) easy-to-use programming language to work with datasets. It can be used with CSV, JSON, and XML files. Python requires a download of the language (www.python.org), and runs on many Windows, Mac, or UNIX systems. You can either write Python in your computer's command line or use a shell.

There are Python libraries that are especially helpful when working with library metadata. Python libraries are a specific set to functions and methods that allow you to perform actions without writing your own code. For instance, the lxml library is intended for use with XML files. PyMarc is a Python library for working with MARC21 bibliographic data. According to the PyMarc GitHub documentation, PyMarc "provides an API for reading, writing and modifying MARC records. It was mostly designed to be an emergency eject seat, for getting your data assets out of MARC and into some kind of saner representation."

As with XSLT, library organizations regularly host workshops and webinars for learning Python in a library context. For a general understanding of Python, there are a number of tutorials online and beginner books are available through libraries.

METADATA HARVESTING

Implementing metadata standards used across the cultural heritage community allows for opportunities to share metadata in large databases. This data can "play well" with others, since they are formatted the same way. The large databases (such as DPLA) can harvest data from individual repositories to create a large dataset where researchers can search across repositories to find relevant resources.

OAI-PMH

The Open Archives Initiative Protocol for Metadata Harvesting (OAI-PMH) is a protocol developed specifically for harvesting cultural heritage metadata and uses Simple Dublin Core as its minimum standard. Repositories may expose all or some of their metadata for metadata harvesting, and many digital repository systems have OAI-PMH capabilities built into them. If a repository has metadata in a different standard (i.e., MODS), the repository must map and crosswalk the data to Dublin Core before exposing it for harvesting. This may mean some fields are dropped to simplify the Dublin Core made available for harvesting. The harvested metadata can be compiled into aggregator sites.

DPLA

The Digital Public Library of America (DPLA) is the main aggregator site in the United States for digital cultural heritage objects. Launched in 2013, DPLA harvests metadata for photographs, books, maps, news footage, oral histories, personal letters, museum objects, artwork, government documents, and more. Contributing institutions range from the very large to small historical societies and libraries throughout the country. DPLA harvests metadata and thumbnail and then provides a link to the contributing repository for the fuller metadata record and for viewing the full-size digital object.

CONCLUSION

Metadata work requires working knowledge of many standards. Although it can be tempting to create your own local standards rather than taking the time to learn the national standards, creating standardized description saves time in the long run because you can reuse it in various systems and platforms. There are many resources and tutorials available online on all of the standards discussed in this chapter. The source list below offers a few articles and websites to review for more information on metadata standards and principles.

REFERENCES

Baca, Murtha, ed., *Introduction to metadata* (Los Angeles: Getty Research Institute, 2008).

Coyle, Karen, "Understanding Metadata and its Purpose," *The Journal of Academic Librarianship,* 31, no. 2 (2005): 160-163, doi: https://doi .org/10.1016/j.acalib.2004.12.010.

Hillmann, Diane I., Rebecca Guenther, and Allene Hayes. Metadata standards & applications. (Washington, D.C.: Library of Congress, 2008), www.loc .gov/catworkshop/courses/metadatastandards/pdf/MSTraineeManual.pdf.

Riley, Jen, "Understanding Metadata: what is metadata and what is it for?" NISO Primer Series, 2017, https://groups.niso.org/apps/group_public/ download.php/17446/Understanding%20Metadata.pdf.

Taylor, Stephanie. "An Introduction to Dublin Core: tutorial for DCMI Conference The Hague," DCMI International Conference Tutorials, September 21, 2011, http://dublincore.org/resources/training/dc-2011/ Tutorial_Taylor.pdf.

W3 Schools. Online Web Tutorials, accessed May 24, 2018, https://www .w3schools.com.

NOTES

1. Anne J. Gilliland, "Setting the Stage" in *Introduction to Metadata,* ed. Murtha Baca (Los Angeles:Getty Research Institute, 2016), 2.

2. Text Encoding Initiative, www.tei-c.org/index.xml.

3. "Example: Speaker," Text Encoding Initiative, www.tei-c.org/release/doc/ tei-p5-doc/en/html/examples-speaker.html.

4. Library of Congress, MODS Metadata Object Descriptive Schema Official Website, www.loc.gov/standards/mods.

5. JSON-LD website, www.json-ld.org.

CHAPTER FIVE

Things You Might Encounter

This chapter highlights the types of materials you're likely to encounter as a sudden CML. For the sake of readability, we've done our best to structure each section below as follows:

1. Brief description
2. Preferred sources of information
3. Unique descriptive metadata elements and their respective MARC field
4. Special considerations
5. Helpful resources with examples

MONOGRAPHS

Brief description

Monographs are the most common item that catalogers create records for. Monographs can be issued all at once, or over time, but in

either case they are generally conceived and planned as single literary units. For this reason, there is a one-to-one relationship between records and monographs in most catalogs and discovery environments.

Another feature that characterizes monographs is that they are
frequently re-issued over long periods of time. This can happen for
various reasons, and CMLs generally try to distinguish between
republication events that merely reflect a new *printing* or *manu-
facture* of the same text, and those that reflect substantive changes
to the text itself. Often, in the world of monographic publications, a
change to the text is referred to as a new edition; it gets a new record
if it has a different date, page count, or other new distinguishing
change to its production. A reprinting of the same edition by the same
publisher, even if in a slightly different format (such as paperback
instead of hardback) will usually not require a new record. (For
more on differences in content—FRBR works and expressions—and
differences in physical form—FRBR manifestations—see Chapter 2.)

Preferred sources of information

Because monographs are "self-describing"—that is to say, they tend
to carry bibliographic information about themselves somewhere on
the resource—preference is always given to information printed on
(or attached to) the document itself. Monographs have a few common
places where such information may be found, and chief among
these, supported by both tradition and common sense, is the title
page itself. Most descriptive rules, such as RDA and DCRMB, which
are discussed in this volume, require a fairly strict transcription of
information appearing on the title page, even down to recording
typos that appear on a title page as-is. If required information about
a resource cannot be located on its title page, or if the resource lacks
a title page altogether, cataloging codes provide lists of alternative
sources of information, usually: title page verso and other preliminary
pages (e.g., a half title or series title, acknowledgements, forewords,
etc.); other places within the resource itself, such as captions,
afterwords, or the colophon, which, when present, appears on the
final leaf of the book; and finally, information appearing on covers,
wrappers, etc. affixed to the book by the manufacturer.

When information cannot be located on the resource itself, it
must be supplied from an external source such as a reference work, a

manufacturer's catalog or website, or even a helpful reference librarian with expertise in the field. In any of these cases, the information is usually marked off so users are aware that it is not inherent to the piece being identified and described.

Descriptive metadata elements

Monographs, being the most common type of resource that libraries collect, tend to form the core of our descriptive rules and practices. Likewise, the majority of our descriptive metadata practice focuses on monographs of various sorts. The basic metadata elements for monographs are those that make up the *ISBD* (see Chapter 3.)

MARC FIELD	ELEMENT
LDR/06	Type of record ("a" for "language material")
LDR/07	Bibliographic level ("m" for "monographic")
020	ISBN
050, 082	Call number (050=LCC; 082=DDC)
100, 110, 111	Author/creator of resource
245	Full title and statement of responsibility
250	Statement of edition or version
260 | 264	Production, publication, distribution, manufacture statements
300	Physical description
500, 505, 510, 520, etc.	Notes
590	Local (copy-specific) notes
600, 610, 611, 630, 650, 651, 655	Subject, genre, etc. controlled terms
700, 710, 711, 730, 740	Other agents related to the resource (e.g., editors, illustrators, etc.), other titles for the resource or its contents
765, 776, 787, etc.	Relationships to other resources (translations, supplements, etc.)
830	Series information

Special considerations

To catalog a monograph in OCLC, use the books template. This will give you pre-filled fixed fields and you will only have to insert the language, country code, and dates. For title, author, publisher, and extent, follow the guidance laid out in earlier chapters.

The notes field is where catalogers get a chance to record interesting observations about the resource, the circumstances under which it has been created, published, or acquired. Some note fields are fairly structured—field 505 for table-of-contents like information typically makes use of ISBD punctuation to provide a structure for users. Other notes are more free-form. MARC field 520 is for books summaries and can include a brief overview of what the item is about. This can also be taken from book reviews, Amazon, or any number of sources; just remember to credit them!

One final note about notes: Keep in mind that typically a record represents a resource as it was (or was intended to be) published. Things that happened to the particular copy of that resource, while perhaps of legitimate interest, need to be specifically noted as copy- or item-specific information; one common way of doing this in MARC is to record the note in field 590 (local information).

In regards to classification and subject headings, remember to class based on either subject or, if it is a novel, by author. Your call number should match the first subject heading. Example: TR145 is the class for books about photography published after 1850. The subject heading would be Photography, which could also be limited by the geographic location covered by the book.

Helpful Resources

Lois Mai Chan, *Cataloging and classification: an introduction*. 4th ed. Lanhan, Md.: Rowman and Littlefield, 2016.

Daniel Joudrey, Arlene G. Taylor, and David Peter Miller, *Introduction to cataloging and classification*. 11th ed. Santa Barbara, CA: Libraries Unlimited, 2015.

Robert L. Maxwell. *Maxwell's handbook for RDA: explaining and illustrating RDA: Resource Description and Access, using MARC21*. Chicago: ALA Editions, 2014.

Florence A. Salinger and Eileen Zagon. *Notes for catalogers: a sourcebook for use with AACR2*. White Plains, N.Y.: Knowledge Industry Publications, 1985.

CONTINUING RESOURCES (PERIODICALS)

In addition to monographs (items that are published once), most institutions collect materials that are published on a regular, ongoing basis. Resources like magazines, journals, and periodicals all fall into this category, which catalogers often refer to as "continuing resources."

Just because something is issued in multiple parts does not mean it is necessarily a continuing resource; many monographic items like encyclopedias and handbooks are issued in multiple volumes, sometimes over a long period of time. They can nonetheless be treated, for cataloging purposes, as parts of a monograph (see above). Serials, or continuing resources, are characterized by the fact that, while they are being issued, they have no *predetermined* conclusion. This does not mean, of course, than no continuing resource ever ends (some, in fact, end after only a single issue) but rather the intentions of a resources publisher is for it to continue.

Because of their somewhat ephemeral nature, providing accurate metadata for continuing resources is challenging and typically involves the collective curation of metadata. Records for serials are frequently edited as new facts about a publication come to light or as changes occur. One of the great challenges in managing serial publications is, of course, their tendency to change; determining how to deal with a particular change in the title or other descriptive element of a continuing resource. Some changes may be accounted for by modifying existing descriptions; others may be considered significant enough to create a whole new description.

The primary specialist community for serials cataloging in North America is called CONSER (Cooperative Online Serials) and is run under the auspices of the Program for Cooperative Cataloging (PCC). Instructions for describing continuing resources are scattered throughout RDA. As a result, a more useful resource, if available, can be found in the CONSER Cataloging Manual (CCM). Ed Jones's *RDA and Serials Cataloging* is also a standard and extremely useful resource.

Preferred sources of information

Because serials are really collections of smaller resources, issued over a stretch of time, the question of what sources to use when describing them inevitably turns on the question of when. That is to say, when discussing how to describe a serial or other continuing resources, CMLs typically want to look for the *first*, or at least *earliest* part of the serial they can find, and use that at the chief source of information. Changes that occur over time are then compared with this first issue; in some circumstances, the changes are great enough to call for a new descriptive altogether, at which point this new issue becomes the *first/earliest* and hence the basis of the description.

It is not, of course, always possible to identify the first or earliest issue of serial clearly; some resources—often called "integrating resources"—undergo a process of continual updating and replacement of contents such that it may be impossible for the CML to find traces of earlier versions.

As is the case with monographs (discussed above), when necessary information about the resource cannot be found anywhere "on the pieces," it may be supplied from reference sources, and when this occurs the information is generally marked off so users can tell it was supplied from some other source.

Descriptive metadata elements of CRs

In MARC, records for serials are clearly distinguishable from their monographic counterparts by a fixed field in the Leader area (LDR07, "Bibliographic level," set to "s"). Nonetheless they use most of the same MARC fields such as 245 for title, 250 for edition, 264 for publication, and 300 for physical description. Some fields, on the other hand, are unique to serials records.

MARC	VALUE
LDR/07	Bibliographic level ("s" for "serial")
310	Frequency
321	Former frequency
362	Sequential designations

The three fields above are descriptive fields that enable CMLs to record information about the ongoing history of the serial. Catalogers are often interested in recording information about a serial's frequency (how often it is issued) and regularity (whether its publication pattern varies). More importantly, however, CMLs who work with continuing resources are very interested in determining a serials "designations"—that is, how the serial divides itself up as its issued. For example, does each part of the serial call itself "volume X" (a numeric designation), does it call itself "March 2018" (a chronological designation), or—as is perhaps most common—does it use multiple systems: "Volume 1, issue 3 (March 2018)?" This information is important to users and other catalogers alike as it plays a role both in the acquisition and receipt of journal issues as well as the ongoing maintainance of the serial's metadata. In addition, to record a serial's designations, the 362 field is important because it typically represents the information that was found on the first or earliest available issue.

Helpful Resources

Anglo-American Cataloging Rules, 2nd edition, revised. Chicago: ALA, 2002. Chapter 12, Continuing resources.

CONSER cataloging manual (CCM). Washington, D.C.: CONSER. Available through *Cataloger's Desktop*; frequently updated.

Ed Jones, *RDA and serials cataloging*. Chicago: ALA Editions, 2013.

AUDIOVISUAL MATERIALS

We've chosen to lump together audiovisual materials to include any resource possessing audio and/or visual components. While there are notable distinctions between describing audio versus audiovisual materials, we are choosing to highlight similarities to be concise and let readers explore the helpful resources noted below to better understand those differences. Some examples include spoken word recordings, music, film and video games. These materials are packaged in a variety of different formats (DVD, CD, .mp3, .mp4, etc.) and often require special equipment or system requirements to use them.

Due to the increased use of non-textual media in society and their incorporation into technological platforms, describing audiovisual materials exhaustively and accurately is quite challenging.

Unfortunately, choosing the source of information for AV materials is not a straightforward process and takes experience to get fully comfortable with. Due to the variability one can encounter with media materials, there are often various considerations a CML needs to assess before selecting the preferred source of information for transcription purposes. For instance, preferred sources of information for recorded music tend to change whether the resource is issued as a single unit or if it has more than one part.[1] The preferred source of information for video, on the other hand, is the title frames of the video itself first and foremost.[2] While it takes some getting used to, the referenced guides in consultation with Chapter 2 of RDA should inform you accordingly.

When continuing the description process, please keep in mind the following metadata fields when describing AV materials that you may not encounter with other resources:

DESCRIPTION	MARC FIELD
Type of Visual Material	008(33)
Equipment or System Requirement	538
Note on Title	500
Place and Date of Capture	518
Medium of Performance of Musical Content	500
Language and Accessibility of Content	546
Supplementary Content	504, 500
Performers, Narrators, Presenters	511
Artistic and Technical Credits	508
Notes on Production, Publication, Distribution, Manufacturing, and Copyright	500
Summary of Content	520
Intended Audience	521
Awards	586

Further, the MARC 006, 007, and 008 fields record some of the most important AV attributes such as language, publication date (or date of distribution, release, reissue, etc.), country of publication, duration, target audience, category of material, color, dimensions, base material, type of recording, playing speed, and configuration of playback channels. When working with non-MARC metadata, the descriptive elements found within these fields remain extremely important; they should be identified, described accurately, and be distinguishable from one another. Inputting and checking this data can be quite tedious, but it is generally easier to query for reporting purposes and enhancing discoverability. Please pay close attention to all of the above metadata elements.

While there are numerous special considerations unique to AV materials, we'd like to highlight one other that merits mentioning in this brief overview: Multiple Pieces, Accompanying Materials & Bound-withs. There is perhaps nothing more frustrating about processing AV materials than the proliferation of pieces, accompanying materials, and bibliographic records needed to fully describe the item in hand. Depending on your institution's circulation and cataloging policies, this could mean a lot of extra work both describing the record and processing the materials. Compared to other formats found in this chapter, (except for kits) this aspect of AV description and processing requires close attention to detail to ensure the resource(s) in hand are appropriately discoverable and able to be circulated.

Helpful Resources

OLAC's Best Practices for Cataloging DVD-Video and Blu-Ray Discs[3]

OLAC's Best Practices for Cataloging Streaming Media[4]

OLAC's Best Practices for Cataloging Video Games[5]

ALA's RDA Webinars for:

Special formats (DVDs, kits, etc.)[6]

Music - Basic Overview[7]

Music—Scores[8]

Music—Sound recordings[9]
Oral Histories[10]
MLA's Webinar for:

Cataloging Music Basics[11]

Cataloging Music AV[12]
Music Cataloging at Yale[13]

GRAPHIC MATERIALS

Non-projected graphic materials are typically defined as being two-dimensional objects or documents in the form of pictures, photographs, posters, and artwork. Cartographic materials generally encompass maps, atlases, globes, digital cartographic items, aerial photographs, and satellite images. Like the audiovisual materials section above, we are choosing to lump these materials together to highlight similarities even though we recognize that there are real distinctions between describing non-projected graphic materials and cartographic materials. And due to the equally diverse nature of these types of materials, describing them accurately (specifically cartography) takes time and experience.

Before you begin describing any graphic materials, it's always helpful to spend a couple of minutes examining and familiarizing yourself with the object in front of you, noting the presence or absence of titles, statements of responsibility, dates, etc. Then, you'll need to decide which of the two main description standards (RDA and DCRM) will be used for describing those graphic materials. Some considerations when deciding which standard to use include:

> **Cataloger knowledge of the different standards—**RDA is usually more familiar, and thus, easier to implement.

> **Level of description desired—**DCRM includes information not required by RDA such as more precise physical descriptions.

> **Likelihood of different manifestations–**DCRM facilitates deciphering between different manifestations by

including more precise descriptions of physical characteristics. This is important for rare materials in particular.

Since many graphic materials do not contain titles, (i.e., personal photographs) preferred sources of information may not be available, leaving the cataloger responsible for title creation. Alternatively, other graphic materials have multiple titles (i.e., travel map pamphlets), so selecting the primary title and the secondary titles often have a preferred order. For example, for cartographic materials the preferred source of information order is as follows: (1) Title located within the neat line or border of the main map; (2) Title from the recto but outside the neat line or border of the main map; (3) Panel title; (4) Title from verso of the cartographic image; (5) Title from cover, container, envelope, etc. While it takes some getting used to, the referenced guides in consultation with DCRM or Chapter 2 of RDA should inform you accordingly.

When continuing the description process, please keep in mind the following metadata fields when describing graphic materials that you may not encounter with other resources:

DESCRIPTION	MARC FIELD
Coded Cartographic Mathematical Data (coordinates & scale)	034, 255
Geographic Area Code	043
Geographic Classification	52
Physical Medium	340
Geospatial Reference Data (projection, scale factor, etc.)	008(22-23), 342
Relief Note	008(18-21), 500
Geographic Coverage Note	522

Like audiovisual materials, the elements contained MARC 006, 007, and 008 fields record some of the most important descriptive attributes, such as type of record, type of visual material, specific material designation, color, primary support material, secondary support material, and remoting sensing image information. When working with non-MARC metadata, the descriptive elements found within these fields remain extremely important; they should be identified, described accurately, and be distinguishable from one another. Inputting and checking this data can be quite tedious, but it is generally easier to query for reporting purposes and enhancing discoverability. Please pay close attention to all of the above metadata elements when describing graphic materials.

While there are numerous special considerations unique to graphic materials, we'd like to highlight one specifically that merits mentioning in this brief overview: Subject Headings and Genre/Form Terms. Since the titles of graphic materials can vary wildly, making sure users can either collate or browse related items easily is essential for such collections. As such, assigning accurate topical subject headings, classification numbers, and genre/form headings is an important step of graphic materials description and discovery. Resources to keep in mind when applying subject headings, classification numbers, and genre/form headings for cartographic resources include the Library of Congress Class G schedule, which is comprised of up to two cutters in order to capture the hierarchies present. When applying call numbers, it is often helpful to perform browse searches of similar collections so you can double-check your work. Finally, you may want to consider expanding your controlled genre/form vocabulary beyond Library of Congress to include Getty's ATT terms.

Helpful Resources

The Association of Canadian Map Libraries and Archives (ACMLA) "Cataloging Toolkit" (www.acmla.org/tools.html).

The Map Cataloger's Toolbox (www.acsu.buffalo.edu/~dbertuca/maps/cat/map-cat-toolbox.html).

The Map Librarian's Toolbox, (www.waml.org/maptools.html #mapcat).

RDA & Maps: www.ala.org/alcts/confevents/upcoming/webinar/cat/092811.

Larsgaard, Mary Lynette. *Map Librarianship: An Introduction.* 3rd ed. Englewood, Colo.: Libraries Unlimited, 1998.

Paige G. Andrew, Susan M. Moore, and Mary Lynette Larsgaard. *RDA and Cartographic Resources.* Chicago, IL: ALA Editions, 2015.

Robinson, Arthur H., Morrison, Joel L., Muehrcke, Phillip C., Kimerling, A. John, and Guptil, Stephen C. *Elements of Cartography.* 6th ed. New York: John Wiley & Sons, 1995.

Robert L. Maxwell. *Maxwell's Handbook for RDA: Explaining and Illustrating RDA: Resource Description and Access Using MARC21.* London: Facet, 2014, Appendix G.

Association of College and Research Libraries. *Descriptive Cataloging of Rare Materials.* Chicago: Rare Books and Manuscripts Section of the Association of College and Research Libraries, 2013.

KITS, ARTIFACTS, AND REALIA

Cataloging three-dimensional objects can present a departure from the cataloging of other resources more commonly found in libraries, including books, journals, and electronic resources. Three-dimensional objects can leave a lot of room for discretion when deciding how to describe that object, especially when it is a naturally-occurring object or specimen that doesn't include a title, author, or place of publication! Since there is such a wide variety of possibilities when it comes to cataloging physical objects, we will focus the following discussion on some common threads and major areas to address and provide some helpful resources where you can learn more about the cataloging of physical objects if they come up in the course of your work.

THREE-DIMENSIONAL OBJECTS

When we talk about physical objects, what do we mean? This category of resources can include anything from a Civil War cannonball to a moth specimen to a sculpture. Anything that a library wishes to include in its collection can indeed be cataloged. The term "realia" is often used to describe these types of resources and applies to both naturally-occurring objects and to "artifacts," or man-made objects.

Many libraries also lend library equipment to patrons, ranging from laptop computers to smartphone chargers to packets of markers. There is great variety in the way in which they choose to catalog these resources and make them discoverable. Some libraries don't catalog them at all; instead preferring to use a dedicated equipment management system rather than the library catalog. Other libraries opt to create brief records rather than full catalog records since these resources are generally intended for in-house use and aren't shared with other libraries through cooperative cataloging or interlibrary loan.

Regardless of whether the object is natural or man-made, the greatest areas of attention for the cataloger are likely to be the physical description and notes fields. Many other areas of the bibliographic record, such as the title and place of publication, look much the same as they would when cataloging a book. The chief source of information for your cataloging will be the item itself along with any accompanying materials. In many cases, as with a naturally-occurring object, there will be little or no written information available, and the CML will have to devise the metadata. When describing a non-labeled hand puppet in the shape of a fox, for example, you may have to simply create a title of *Fox hand puppet*.

Below are some important MARC fields for cataloging physical objects:

DESCRIPTION OF THE FIELD	MARC FIELD
TITLE ■ Some manufactured objects, like board games, will come with a standard title to use when cataloging. ■ Natural specimens and other objects may lack a title; the CML will have to devise a descriptive title for the item.	245
PUBLICATION/DISTRIBUTION ■ This field describes the date and location of creation and the publisher/producer. ■ You may only know some of this information, depending on the item at hand; give what you know.	264
PHYSICAL DESCRIPTION ■ **$a, *extent***: give the number and name of the parts and pieces. If the number of pieces is unknown or difficult to describe you can use *various pieces*. ■ **$b, *other physical details***: give the type of material and color(s). ■ **$c, *dimensions***: give the dimension of the object(s) in centimeters. ■ If the work is inside a container you can give just the dimensions of the container or list the dimensions of the items and note that they are *in container* of given dimensions.	300

DESCRIPTION OF THE FIELD	MARC FIELD
PHYSICAL DESCRIPTION (cont.) ■ *$e, accompanying materials*: list any accompanying items like a booklet that goes with a game. ■ *Example:* **a red coffee mug in a box:** 1 coffee mug; ceramic, red ; 15 x 10 x 10 cm in container 20 x 15 x 15 cm	
RDA CONTENT[14] ■ Likely options include three-dimensional form, tactile three-dimensional form, or cartographic three-dimensional form (for globes and similar resources).	336
RDA MEDIA ■ Most likely *unmediated*	337
RDA CARRIER ■ Most likely *object*	338
GENERAL NOTES ■ *Examples:* a brief description of the work, or the source of the title if taken from an external source or devised by the cataloger.	500
CONTENTS OF THE WORK [if formal contents are given]	505
SUMMARY OF THE WORK	520

KITS

Kits are basically packages of multiple physical items that are cataloged together as a single resource. In AACR2 there were two formal definitions for kits, and "kit" was given its own General Material Designation. Since GMDs are no longer used in RDA, the concept of a kit is now a bit less well-defined. However, the concepts embedded in the AACR2 definitions can still be helpful when cataloging these types of resources:

1. An item containing two or more categories of material, no one of which is identifiable as the predominant constituent of the item.
2. A single-medium package of textual materials.

The first definition provides the most common description of a kit. Essentially it is a resource with multiple physical parts, and none of the parts is the predominant part. If you are describing a work with a dominant part and several supporting parts, this would not be a kit but rather a single item with accompanying materials. The term "kit" is used when there are multiple items and they all have co-equal importance. Some examples might include a kit of whiteboard supplies (markers, eraser, cleaning fluid) or an assessment kit for occupational therapy students that includes several manipulatable items, an instruction manual, and patient forms. The second definition describes a subset of kits that includes only multiple textual items, such as a press kit or a set of printed test materials.

It is also important to distinguish between a *kit* and a *collection*. Whereas a kit is comprised of multiple pieces that constitute a single work/resource, a collection is a *group of multiple works* that are brought together, or collected, so they can be accessed and used more conveniently. As an example, a kit might be a box of whiteboard supplies, and a collection might comprise a set of multiple whiteboard kits and other related equipment housed together at the circulation desk for checkout.

When cataloging kits, the general rules for three-dimensional objects apply as discussed above. In addition, some further cataloging considerations include:

DESCRIPTION OF THE FIELD	MARC FIELD
PHYSICAL DESCRIPTION (several approaches) ■ If you wish to thoroughly describe each component in the kit, provide an *extent, other physical details,* and *dimensions* for each item using a separate 300 field. ■ If you want to be more concise, give the extent of each item (1 instruction manual, 2 DVDs, etc.) and describe any container in the dimensions subfield. ■ If there are a number of heterogeneous materials, you could simply use "various pieces" for the extent.	300

RDA CONTENT, MEDIA, AND CARRIER
■ This section can be tricky due to the multiple pieces in the kit.
■ Preferred Method:
   ❑ Give a separate 336, 337, and 338 for each piece.
   ❑ Each line would start with a $3 indicating which piece the line pertains to.
	336, 337, 338

DESCRIPTION OF THE FIELD	MARC FIELD

Preferred Method (cont.)
 	
  ☐ Example: If the kit includes a DVD and an instruction booklet, you would have **336 $3 DVD video $a moving image; 336 $3 instruction booklet $a text** and then corresponding 337 and 338 fields for each item.
 	
 ▪ Alternate Method:
  ☐ Use only one field each of 336, 337, and 338 and include multiple subfield *a*'s in each line, where each $a relates to one kit component.	

GENERAL DESCRIPTION	500
FORMAL CONTENTS	505
RESTRICTIONS ON USE ▪ Examples include "for in-house use only" or "may only be checked out by children".	506
SUMMARY	520
AUDIENCE ▪ Used if an audience is specified on the kit, e.g. "intended for children ages 6 and up".	521
COPY BEING DESCRIBED ▪ Note any special characteristics of *these items* that distinguish them from other kits of the same manifestation.	590

Helpful Resources

Elrod, J. M. (2015). Kit cataloguing. Retrieved from http://special
-cataloguing.com/node/1414.

Olson, N. B. (2008). *Cataloging of audiovisual materials and other
special materials: A manual based on AACR2 and MARC 21*
(5th ed.). Westport, CT: Libraries Unlimited.

Weber, M. B., & Austin, F. A. (2011). *Describing electronic, digital,
and other media using AACR2 and RDA: A how-to-do-it
manual and CD-ROM for librarians.* New York: Neal-Schuman
Publishers.

Cataloging Three-Dimensional Objects and Kits with RDA: www
.ala.org/alcts/confevents/upcoming/webinar/cat/032812.

RARE BOOKS

What makes cataloging rare books different from "normal" books is that both the content and book itself is cataloged (often called the container). Rare book catalogers not only document the title, author, and subject covered in an item like a non-rare book would be, but we also catalog the binding, provenance, individuals (beyond the author and publisher) involved in the creation of the book as an object (bookbinders, sellers, illustrator, etc.).

This is done for multiple reasons. Like all other materials, we do this to secure the discoverability of all aspects of this object. We also catalog such details of provenance, binding for preservation and security reasons. By detailing what makes a library's copy unique, the library is then able to trace their copy in case of theft, defacement, or damage due to fire, water, or other disaster.

This sort of cataloging will take more in-depth training to learn the terminology as well as the unique nature of the materials being cataloged. The following provides a very brief overview and includes a listing of some continuing resources for you to further explore.

Describing the Book as an Object

For the most part, cataloging rare books follows the same fixed and variable fields discussed above in the Monographs section. The one different is described below: the local notes.

Local Notes in the Master Record

The most important rule for rare book and special collections cataloging is: never put in the master record what is only about your copy. Your book may be bound in leather but another institution is in morocco. Your donor and provenance information is specific to the copy you have in your hand. All of the following sections (provenance, binding, condition) belong in a local variable field, usually in the 59X range. Some libraries place all binding notes in their 590, donor notes in 591, and so on. Consistency is what is key here—you want the same note in the same field for each individual item.

Provenance

Provenance is the history of humans involvement with a certain object. Examples of provenance include: bookplates, signatures, inscriptions, marginalia, and any other marking on the item that was included after production (such as booksellers or binders tickets). This also allows for tracking donors—who gifted the item or collection to your institution. This is helpful to research for those are interested in a donor's library.

Binding Notes

Rare book catalogers include binding notes in the local record. As discussed above, this covers the condition of the book as well as provenance. This also includes the type of binding the book resides in. There are multiple types of binding: leather (treated cowskin), morocco (treated goatskin), cloth, and linson (paper stamped to look like cloth). A full list with descriptions can be found in the AbeBooks "Guide to Understanding Bindings" (www.abebooks.com/books/rarebooks/collecting-guide/understanding-rare-books/understanding-bindings.shtml).

The level of detail noted in this local note is up to the cataloger or institution. Some can be simple: institution copy in blue cloth with provenance markings of former owner. Others can be more detailed and describe the intricate decorations used to make a binding more attractive. For detailed definitions and descriptions of parts of the book consult: *ABC for Booksellers* by John Carter, which is available online in PDF form.

Example of binding note: Gift of [donor name], [date]. Bound in full calf leather. Seven raised bands on spine. Title and decorations tooled in gilt on spine. Top edge gilt; fore and bottom edges untrimmed. Marbled endpapers in purple, red, and green. Former owner's bookplate (image of a wolf head with 'Jack London' above surrounded by dog sled handle) on front pastedown.

Condition

Recording condition at the point of cataloging tracks how the book was received. If inventory is conducted later, the current condition can be checked against the original condition and the judgement can be made if the condition has deteriorated. This can happen for three reasons: theft, defacement, or physical deterioration due to fire, water, or other environmental reason. Theft—Has the book gone missing from its place on the shelf? Defacement—Have pages been torn, plates or other illustrations removed, etc.? Physical deterioration—Has red rot infected a leather binding? Has your roof sprung a leak, allowing the paper to become waterlogged? All of this impacts the insurance your institution has to cover the cost of the collections it houses and is meant to protect.

Genre Terms and Relationship Designators

Genre terms from the LCGFT are allowable in rare materials records but AAT, RBMS genre terms were created with specific definitions in mind that LCGFT simply do not encompass. These reflect binding, printing, and provenance specific to your institution copy.

The two most followed are the Rare Books and Manuscripts Section (RBMS) of ALA (http://rbms.info/vocabularies/index.shtml) and the Art and Architecture Thesaurus (AAT) from the Getty Institute (www.getty.edu/research/tools/vocabularies/aat). These cover everything from bindings (leather, morocco, etc.) to provenance (author's signed copy, etc.) to formats (photographs, etc.). These are described more in Chapter 3.

ARCHIVAL COLLECTIONS

An archival collection is a group of materials coming from one source or encompassing one specific topic. Most frequently, these materials are papers consisting of correspondence and other records. Photographs, ephemera, realia, and more can also be included. This is the one time that local notes are allowed in the master record—the entire record is based on a completely unique collection and therefore every field is local in that sense.

To catalog an archival collection, a finished finding aid will provide the most accurate information that can be then reflected in the catalog record. A finding aid is detailed inventory that lists box and folder content and is arranged by a national standard called *Describing Archives: A Content Standard* (DACS). Cataloging an archival collection without one is possible but requires a great deal of work on the cataloger's part.

Fields for Archival Collections

FIXED FIELD	CODE	DESCRIPTION
Rec type	p	(mixed or visual materials)
Bib level	c	collection
Srce	d	Other cataloging source (e.g. not Library of Congress)
Enc level		Dependent on local practice
Desc	i	i for RDA
Date	i	Inclusive (earliest date first, then latest)
Country	xx	Do not identify a country unless all materials were created in one place

VARIABLE FIELD	FIELD TITLE	NOTES
046	Date field	Take from dates in fixed fields. Example: inclusive dates are 1945-1987, 046 $k 1945 $l 1987 $2 edtf
100/110	Main access point	Whomever is the sole entity or person responsible for creating the collection
245	Title for the collection	Archivist created title *Example:* Joe Smith papers; Smith Corporation records
264	Dates of creation	Inclusive dates from the date fields, bulk dates are not always present *Example:* 1945-1987 (bulk 1945-1950)
300	Extent	Number of items/boxes/cubic feet (can be repeated for different measurement) *Example:* 2 cubic feet (3 boxes)
500	General notes	

(cont.)

VARIABLE FIELD	FIELD TITLE	NOTES
506	Restrictions on access	Describes the accessibility of the materials Example: Materials are located offsite. Access to originals restricted due to preservation issues.
520	Scope and content note	Summary of what the collection contains
540	Reproduction and digitization restrictions or permission	Explains if the materials are not open to the public or if there are rights issues Example: Creator's rights not transferred to institution. Digitization not allowed.
541	Acquisition	Donor, gift, or purchase note
545	Biographical or historical note	Describes the main access point and how they were related to the collection
561	Custodial history	Explains transfers from other departments if materials were separated, etc.

Helpful Resources

For a complete guide to the marriage of DACS and RDA, please see the following resources:

Nimer, Cory. Archival materials: Using RDA with DACS . Retrieved from http://youtu.be/n5fY9L9zZcM.

Nimer, Cory. RDA and Archives. *Journal of Archival Organization*, 8(3–4), 2010, 227–243.

Thurman, A. C. FRBR and archival materials: Collections and context, not works and content. In A. G. Taylor (Ed.), *Understanding FRBR: What it is and how it will affect our retrieval tools*, (pp. 99–100). Westport, CT: Libraries Unlimited, 2007.

DIGITAL COLLECTIONS

Cataloging digital items is very similar to cataloging the physical version of the same resource, including images, textual documents, and audiovisual files. Due to the similarities with the physical formats described above, this section on cataloging digital collections will focus more on non-MARC metadata records, specifically Dublin Core and MODS. Additional information about these metadata schemas can be found in Chapter 4.

Fields for Digital Collections Metadata

MARC FIELD	DUBLIN CORE FIELD	MODS FIELD
245	Title	titleInfo
1XX	Creator	name
6XX	Subject	subject, classification
300, 5XX	Description	abstract, note, tableOfContents
264 $a $b	Publisher	originInfo/publisher
7XX	Contributor	name
264 $c	Date	originInfo/dateIssued
LDR06, LDR07, 655	Type	typeOfResource, genre
340, 856 $q	Format	physicalDescription
010, 020, 022, 024, 856 $u	Identifier	identifier
534 $t, 786 $o $t	Source	relatedItem
008 [35-37]	Language	language
530, 760, 787	Relation	relatedItem
6XX $y, 651	Coverage	subject/temporal, subject/cartographics
506, 540	Rights	accessCondition

Crosswalks and Application Profiles

Many crosswalks between these different schemas exist. Some widely used crosswalks from the Library of Congress include:

MARC to Dublin Core Crosswalk (www.loc.gov/marc/ marc2dc.html).

Dublin Core Metadata Element Set Mapping to MODS Version 3 (www.loc.gov/standards/mods/dcsimple -mods.html)

MARC 21 to MODS 3.6 Mapping (www.loc.gov/standards/mods/v3/mods-mapping-3-6.html)

Metadata application profiles are often developed to document how metadata records within a digital repository should be structured, stored, and made available. A few examples of metadata application profiles and best practices include:

Digital Public Library of America's Metadata Application Profile (https://pro.dp.la/hubs/metadata-application-profile)

Cornell University Library's Metadata Application Profiles (https://confluence.cornell.edu/display/mwgweb/CUL+Metadata+Application+Profiles)

Mountain West Digital Library's Dublin Core Application Profile (https://mwdl.org/docs MWDL_DC_Profile_Version_2.0.pdf)

Empire State Digital Network Metadata Requirements (https://empirestate.digital/contributors/metadata-requirements)

Helpful Resources

Digital Public Library of America, Using Metadata to Describe Digital Content (https://pro.dp.la/projects/using-metadata-to-describe-digital-content).

Dublin Core Metadata Initiative, Metadata Training Resources User Guide (http://dublincore.org/resources/training).

Minnesota Metadata Guidelines for Dublin Core Metadata Training Manual (http://mn.gov/bridges/bestprac/training.pdf).

University of Texas Libraries, Metadata Basics LibGuide (http://guides.lib.utexas.edu/metadata-basics/resources-tools).

NOTES

1. Yale University Library, Preferred source of information (RDA 2.1.2.2-3 and 2.2), https://web.library.yale.edu/cataloging/music/prefsource.

2. Yale University Library, RDA Video Checklist (Provisional), www.library
.yale.edu/cataloging/Orbis2Manual/RDA%20video%20checklist.htm.

3. Online Audiovisual Catalogers, Inc., Best Practices for Cataloging DVD-
Video and Blu-ray Discs Using RDA and MARC21, http://olacinc.org/
sites/default/files/DVD_Blu-ray-RDA-Guide-Version-1-1-final-aug2018
-rev-1.pdf.

4. Online Audiovisual Catalogers, Inc., Best Practices for Cataloging
Streaming Media Using RDA and MARC21, http://olacinc.org/sites/
default/files/Streaming_Media_RDA-April2018_a.pdf.

5. Online Audiovisual Catalogers, Inc., Best Practices for Cataloging Video
Games Using RDA and MARC21, http://olacinc.org/sites/default/files/
Video%20Game%20Best%20Practices-April-2018%20Revision-a.pdf.

6. Association for Library Collections and Technical Services, Cataloging
Icky Things, or, If You Can Catalog a Book, You Can Catalog Anything,"
www.ala.org/alcts/confevents/upcoming/webinar/cat/022410ick.

7. Association for Library Collections and Technical Services, RDA Basics
for Music Materials, www.ala.org/alcts/confevents/webinars/041614.

8. Association for Library Collections and Technical Services, RDA and
Music Basics: Scores, 2011, www.ala.org/alcts/confevents/upcoming/
webinar/cat/101911.

9. Association for Library Collections and Technical Services, RDA and
Music Basics, Sound Recordings, 2011, www.ala.org/alcts/confevents/
upcoming/webinar/cat/102611.

10. Association for Library Collections and Technical Services, Doing Oral
History, 2016, www.ala.org/alcts/confevents/upcoming/webinar/042016.

11. Music Library Association, Music Cataloging Basics, 2015, https://vimeo
.com/225164186.

12. Music Library Association, Cataloging Music Audiovisual Materials
Using RDA, 2015, https://vimeo.com/225167889.

13. Yale University Library, Music Cataloging at Yale, https://web.library
.yale.edu/cataloging/music.

14. Complete lists of available Content, Media, and Carrier terms are
available from the Library of Congress's *Value Lists for Codes and
Controlled Vocabularies* (www.loc.gov/standards/valuelist/).

CHAPTER SIX

Tools of the Trade

Knowing the relevant resources available to the cataloging and metadata communities is equally (if not more) important to a sudden CML as understanding the nuances behind resource description theory and end-user search behaviors. Having easy access to the various standards we use and guidance from experts helps to reduce the stress associated with being a sudden CML. Not only do the tools below provide clear examples of the work you'll likely encounter as you begin describing resources, they also give you a reference point if you need to explain your work to others. In general, this chapter tries to provide a comprehensive (but not exhaustive) list of the practical tools of the trade we rely upon to facilitate the resource description process.

WHERE TO FIND . . .

Frameworks

When you hear someone talking about a cataloging, metadata or description framework, think about big picture theories regarding how the bibliographic world operates. Frameworks offer perspectives on the structure of and relationships between bibliographic and authority records, as well as a vocabulary to facilitate the cataloging process.[1] Unlike a standard, a framework does not prescribe rules as to how any given resource should be described. Unlike schemas, they do not prescribe specific formatting rules as to how bibliographic information should be packaged.

Functional Requirements for Bibliographic Records (FRBR)

FRBR was developed by the International Federation of Library Associations and Institutions (IFLA) between 1992-1996. The full report can be found online: www.ifla.org/VII/s13/frbr/frbr.htm or www.ifla.org/VII/s13/frbr/frbr.pdf.[2]

Functional Requirements for Authority Data (FRAD)

Again, developed by IFLA, FRAD is an extension and expansion of the FRBR model or framework, first published in 2008 and last revised in 2013. The full report can be found online: www.ifla.org/files/assets/cataloguing/frad/frad_2013.pdf.

Resource Description Framework (RDF)

Created by the W3C, "RDF is a framework for representing information in the web . . .. The core structure of the abstract syntax is a set of triples, each consisting of a subject, a predicate and an object (www.w3.org/TR/2014/REC-rdf11-concepts-20140225)."[3] W3C also published a schema to facilitate the formatting of RDF, which is known as Resource Description Framework Schema, so RDF qualifies as a hybrid framework-schema (RDFS).

Bibliographic Framework Initiative (BIBFRAME 2.0)

Initiated by the Library of Congress (LOC), BIBFRAME 2.0 is an ambitious initiative that is still a work in progress at the time of this publication. In short, BIBFRAME seeks to incorporate and expand upon the important framework elements found in FRBR, FRAD, and RDF as well as provide a schema to replace MARC21. Like RDF, BIBFRAME, in theory, will be a hybrid framework-schema, built flexibly to work with various description standards. That being said, there are still many unknowns and the date of its potential implementation is unclear. The LOC maintains a website with comprehensive details on the various stages of the initiative (www .loc.gov/bibframe).

Dublin Core (Dublin Core Metadata Initiative (DCMI))

Dublin Core is also a hybrid metadata framework-schema in that it provides a set of eighteen metadata elements alongside schemas to render those elements in XML and RDFS. DCMI does not provide the precise standards on how resources should be described within its set of eighteen elements. Documentation, examples, recommended resources, and guidelines are all freely available online (http:// dublincore.org/documents).

CIDOC Conceptual Reference Model

CIDOC is a framework that largely serves the museum community by providing "definitions and a formal structure for describing the implicit and explicit concepts and relationships used in cultural heritage documentation."[4]

Description Standards

Description standards prescribe a systematic set of rules regarding how resources should be described. Unlike frameworks, standards are less concerned with the big-picture theories of bibliographic structure, relationships, and vocabulary, instead focusing on describing the item in hand. And unlike schemas, standards do not prescribe a specific way in which resource description should be formatted and packaged.

International Standard Bibliographic Description (ISBD)

Produced by IFLA in 2007, ISBD is a set of rules to create bibliographic descriptions in standard form based on nine areas of description: (1) content form and media type area; (2) title and statement of responsibility; (3) edition; (4) material type; (5) publication and distribution information; (6) material description; (7) series information; (8) note fields; and 9) resource identifier and availability. Subsequently, the ISBD Review Group has aligned the rules of ISBD with FRBR, FRAD, and RDA in its most current version (www.ifla .org/files/assets/cataloguing/isbdisbd-cons_20110321.pdf and www .ifla.org/files/assets/cataloguing/isbd/OtherDocumentation/isbd2 rda_alignment_v3_1.pdf).

Resource Description and Access (RDA)

RDA is modeled on the frameworks provided by FRBR and FRAD and was built with enough flexibility to be compatible with existing content schemas (MARC21, MODS, METS, etc.). Originally published as a physical monograph by ALA in 2010, RDA was designed to exist as a digital imprint available via the RDA Toolkit (www.rdatoolkit.org).[5]

Describing Archives: A Content Standards (DACS)

"DACS is an output-neutral set of rules for describing archives, personal papers, and manuscript collections, and can be applied to all material types. It is the U.S. implementation of international standards (i.e., ISAD[G] and ISAAR[CPF]) for the description of archival materials and their creators."[6] The current version of DACS is posted by the Society of American Archivists (SAA) on GitHub. (https://github.com/saa-ts-dacs/dacs) The second edition of DACS is also available on the SAA website (www2.archivists .org/standards/DACS).

Descriptive Cataloging of Rare Materials (DCRM)

DCRM is managed by the Rare Books and Manuscripts Section (RBMS) of the Association of College and Research Libraries (ACRL). DCRM has seven separate manuals that prescribe rules and standards to specific rare material formats such as books, manuscripts, cartography, etc. The manuals are all freely available online in addition to an excellent companion guide that provides thorough examples of how to catalog rare books (http://rbms.info/dcrm/).

Cataloging Cultural Objects (CCO)

CCO is a description standard for the cultural heritage community. The CCO's website is very useful in that it includes the CCO manual, practical examples, and training tools (http://cco.vrafoundation.org).

PREMIS Data Dictionary for Preservation Metadata

PREMIS is an "international standard for metadata to support the preservation of digital objects and ensure their long-term usability."[7] The PREMIS Data Dictionary is freely available online with useful examples and other relevant tools (www.loc.gov/standards/premis).

Content Schemas

Schemas define the structure of content and metadata so that it can be processed by automated computer processes such as data crawling or mining. With content schemas, programmers are able to create more friendly interfaces for the cataloging community, so that we can input metadata while backend scripts encode that metadata according to the prescribed schema in question. Unlike frameworks and standards, schemas are very precise sets of rules used to encode data in a machine readable format.

Machine-Readable Cataloging (MARC21)

MARC21 is a content schema or data format that "provides the mechanism by which computers exchange, use, and interpret bibliographic information, and its data elements make up the foundation of most library catalogs used today."[8] The LOC maintains comprehensive online documentation for all MARC21 fields for bibliographic, authority, holdings, classification, and community records. This freely available documentation is particularly important to sudden catalogers (www.loc.gov/marc).

Metadata Encoding and Transmission Standard (METS)

"The METS schema is a standard for encoding descriptive, administrative, and structural metadata regarding objects within a digital library, expressed using the XML schema language of the W3C. The standard is maintained in the Network Development and MARC Standards Office of the LOC, and is being developed as an initiative of the Digital Library Federation."[9] METS documentation, schema, examples and profiles are all freely available online (www.loc.gov/standards/mets).

Metadata Object Description Schema (MODS)

"The LOC" Network Development and MARC Standards Office, with interested experts, developed the MODS in 2002 for a bibliographic element set that may be used for a variety of purposes, and particularly for library applications. As an XML schema it is intended to be able to carry selected data from existing MARC 21 records as well as to enable the creation of original resource description records."[10] MODS documentation, uses, features, tools, and other valuable information are all freely available online (www.loc.gov/standards/mods).

Metadata Authority Description Schema (MADS)

MADS serves as a companion to MODS, providing an XML schema to record metadata about agents, events, and terms. MADS documentation is also freely available online (www.loc.gov/standards/mads).

Encoded Archival Description (EAD)

"Development of the EAD DTD began with a project initiated by the University of California, Berkeley, Library in 1993. The goal of the Berkeley project was to investigate the desirability and feasibility of developing a nonproprietary encoding standard for machine-readable finding aids such as inventories, registers, indexes, and other documents created by archives, libraries, museums, and manuscript repositories to support the use of their holdings."[11] EAD documentation and other related tools are freely available online (www.loc.gov/ead/index.html).

Encoded Archival Context for Corporate Bodies, Persons, and Families (EAC-CPF)

An XML-schema that "provides a grammar for encoding names of creators of archival materials and related information . . . .. It is used closely in association with Encoded Archival Description (EAD), an XML-Schema for encoding archival finding aids, but not limited to it. In 2011 EAC became an adopted standard of the Society of American Archivists (SAA)."[12] The 2014 edition of EAC-CPF is freely available online (https://eac.staatsbibliothek-berlin.de/schema/tag library/cpfTagLibrary2018_EN.html).

Schema.org

In 2011, major search engines (Google, Yahoo, Bing) launched an initiative to "create and support a common set of schemas for structured data markup on web pages."[13] Creating the schema to mark up a website with metadata about itself allows for search engine spiders and parsers to crawl and index content in a more meaningful way. It was developed using an open source community process, where content was shared and commented on via Github (https:// github.com/schemaorg/schemaorg) and a mailing list (http://lists .w3.org/Archives/Public/public-schemaorg/).

Text Encoding Initiative (TEI) Guidelines

The TEI is a consortium that develops and maintains standards for digital text files. Their website includes the Guidelines themselves as well as a variety of resources and training events (www.tei-c.org/ index.xml).

Authority Files and Controlled Vocabularies

Authority files and controlled vocabularies help the cataloging and metadata communities keep like-minded information collated and linked together while trying to avoid duplication of efforts. Think of how many individuals named John Smith have contributed to history, the number of synonyms there are for search term 'Therapeutics,' or what the precise genre form 'Coming-of-age films' should take. Without authority files and controlled vocabularies to guide input consistency, all of the frameworks, standards and schemas discussed above would be rendered useless due to endless variability of name forms and likeminded words.

Library of Congress Authorities and Controlled Vocabularies*

The LOC maintains extensive authority files and controlled vocabularies such as Name Authority File (NAF), Subject Headings (LCSH),

Genre/Form Terms (LCGFT), Demographic Group Terms (LCDGT), and the Thesaurus for Graphic Materials (TGM). The Library of Congress authority search portal is an essential tool for any sudden cataloger (http://authorities.loc.gov). Some important documents related to the LOC authorities are the *Subject Headings Manual*, the *NACO Participants Manual*, and the *SACO Participants Manual*.

Medical Subject Headings (MeSH)

The National Library of Medicine (NLM) maintains its own subject headings, MeSH. "It consists of sets of terms naming descriptors in a hierarchical structure that permits searching at various levels of specificity."[14] The NLM offers a comprehensive search portal of MeSH terms on its website (https://meshb.nlm.nih.gov/search) as well as extensive documentation, helpful tutorials, downloadable files of MeSH in full and relevant presentations, and publications by MeSH staff (www.nlm.nih.gov/mesh).

Geographic Names Information System (GNIS)

Developed by the United States Geological Survey (USGS) in cooperation with the United States Board of Geographic Names (BNG), the GNIS is the official system to query federally authorized geographic names. It is a freely available online service (https://geonames.usgs .gov), and any person may make inquiries about formal decisions on proposed names (new or existing) and names that are in conflict.

Rare Book and Manuscript Section (RBMS) Controlled Vocabularies

The RBMS of ALA has its own controlled vocabulary to facilitate the retrieval of format, genre and other characteristics of rare books and manuscripts important to the research community. These vocabularies are browsable via the RBMS Controlled Vocabularies website (http://rbms.info/vocabularies/index.shtml) and can be formatted into linked-data friendly elements.

Getty's Thesaurus of Geographic Names (TGN), Art & Architecture Thesaurus (ATT), Cultural Objects Name Authority (CONA), Union List of Artist Names (ULAN)

All of the Getty resources named above serve different purposes but are structured similarly. Collectively they serve the purpose of improving access to information for art, architecture, and other material culture. Since they are structured hierarchically (or faceted) and constructed for allowing linked data uses, the Getty vocabularies can be a powerful tool for facilitating research and enabling discovery of the "objects, artists, concepts, and places important to various disciplines that specialize in art, architecture, and material culture."[15] Each is freely available online where they were published under the Open Data Commons Attribution License (ODC-By) (www .getty.edu/research/tools/vocabularies/aat/about.html).

Cataloging Tools and Guides

OCLC's Connexion & Bibliographic Formats and Standards

OCLC's "Connexion lets you create and edit high-quality bibliographic and authority records and then share them with the entire OCLC cooperative, which benefits libraries around the world."[16] Connexion gives you have the ability to search, create, edit, and duplicate the most comprehensive global library database of MARC records. Within this program there are many valuable tools that can guide the record validation, authority and controlled vocabulary linking, and holdings management processes. Access to OCLC's Connexion does not come cheaply (price varies on institution type and size), but it is a vital tool for any CML who wants to manage their collection and make it publicly discoverable. OCLC's *Bibliographic Formats and Standards* accompanies OCLC's Connexion and serves as an extensive guide on how to structure, code, and input the metadata used in bibliographic records within their database.[17]

RDA Toolkit

The RDA Toolkit was built to accommodate multiple learning styles and is an invaluable resource for anyone cataloging in accordance with RDA.[18] The annual rate for a single-user subscription in 2017 started at $191, depending on the number of simultaneous users.[19]

It is important to note, however, the RDA Toolkit is going through a restructure and redesign (3R Project). Once the 3R project is complete, there will be considerable differences in the rules and rule numbering, as well as how the Toolkit displays information. One significant component of the 3R Project is the implementation of the IFLA Library Reference Model (LRM), which expects to add five new entities to RDA from the LRM: Agent, Collective Agent, Nomen,

Place, and Time-span. Any subsequently updated information about the 3R project can be found on the RDA Toolkit's website.[20]

Cataloger's Desktop

Cataloger's Desktop is a valuable reference tool offered by the LOC at a subscription cost beginning at $525, depending on the number of simultaneous users.[21] It provides electronic access to hundreds of cataloging guides and manuals and other important resources such as AACR2, Library of Congress Rule Interpretations, the Subject Cataloging Manual, CONSER Cataloging Manual, LOC' Cutter Table & Geographic Cutters, and many more. Some of these resources will be discussed in greater depth below. The entire list can be found on their webpage (www.loc.gov/cds/desktop/resourcelist.html).

Classification Web (Class Web)

Class Web is another valuable service provided by the LOC, with subscriptions beginning at $325.[22] Class Web allows you to search, browse, and access all of the LCC schedules and LC Authority files. Being able to search these vast resources electronically is an essential tool for copy and original catalogers. One of its main features is that it correlates LCSH with the respective call number classification, which greatly reduces the amount of time spent assigning call numbers and subject headings, as well as double checking the work of others.

ArchivesSpace (previously Archivist's Toolkit and Archon)

The Archivist's Toolkit and Archon were both open source archival management systems that were superseded in 2014 by Archives-Space, which continues to be open source but is now a web-based platform. "The application is designed to support core functions in archives administration such as accessioning; description and arrangement of processed materials including analog, hybrid, and born-digital content; management of authorities (agents and subjects) and rights; and reference service . . .. The application also functions as a metadata authoring tool, enabling the generation of EAD, MARCXML, MODS, Dublin Core, and METS formatted data."[23]

Catalog Calculator

Developed by Kyle Banerjee, Catalog Calculator (http://calculate .alptown.com) is a fantastic and free online reference tool that simplifies and centralizes heavily-used and hard to remember cataloging tasks. It can create cutter numbers for you. It also offers quick reference to geographic area, country and language codes, RDA content types, fixed field data elements by format (008), LCSH and standard subdivisions by category (subfields v,x,y,z), amongst others.

Program for Cooperative Cataloging (PCC)

The four PCC programs (BIBCO, CONSER, NACO, and SACO) are an "international cooperative effort aimed at expanding access to library collections by providing useful, timely, and cost-effective cataloging that meets mutually-accepted standards of libraries around the world."[24] Through PCC's primary web portal, many valuable resources can be found in the form of decisions, policies, manuals, guidelines, training materials, examples, and more (www .loc.gov/aba/pcc). Some of the resources you should be familiar with include: the Provider-Neutral eResource MARC Guidelines,[25] the BIBCO Standard Record (BSR) RDA Metadata Application Profile,[26] *BIBCO Participants Manual,*[27] *Integrating Resources: A Cataloging Manual* (with excellent examples in IR.17),[28] the *CONSER Cataloging Manual*, and the CONSER Editing Guide.[29] And if you find yourself doing authorities cataloging, the *NACO Participants' Manual* and the *SACO Participants' Manual* are also available through this web portal.

Government Publishing Office (GPO) Cataloging Guidelines

The GPO Cataloging Guidelines website (www.fdlp.gov/cataloging -guidelines) is another good starting point for locating the documentation you'll need to begin cataloging, including examples of bibliographic records and useful resources. Much of the content found here is also available on PCC's website; however, the GPO layout is a bit cleaner and their list of guidelines are narrowed down to the most essential resources.

Metadata Manipulation Tools

There comes a time in the life of a sudden CML when they will have to edit a large number of records to either correct mistakes or enhance records. Editing records by hand in local cataloging systems can be tedious and time consuming. Fortunately, developers working in the cataloging and metadata orbit have created some powerful tools to help you analyze, refine, and edit metadata records in bulk. Below are some of our favorite metadata manipulation tools, most of which happen to be free to use.

MarcEdit

MarcEdit was originally developed by Terry Reese in 1999 to batch update a set of MARC records that had been imported with erroneous call numbers.[30] Since then, Reese has released the tool for public use and has continually updated it with new features in addition to posting helpful tutorials and a knowledgebase of how-to articles (http://marcedit.reeset.net/). In addition to its core function of bulk editing MARC records, MarcEdit can now be used to translate metadata into and out of delimited text formats, convert MARC records into different character sets, harvest OAI metadata, and more. It has gained wide acceptance in the metadata community for its ability to quickly perform tasks like adding new fields to a batch of MARC records that would otherwise take hours to perform manually.

OpenRefine

Beginning as a product of Metaweb Technologies in 2010 and then spending two years under Google, OpenRefine is now an open source, community-driven client application designed for exploring and cleaning large datasets[31] (www.openrefine.org). You can use OpenRefine to analyze datasets and look for patterns/insights, cleanup data that may have formatting inconsistencies or other problems, reconcile data and match it with a database, and more. OpenRefine is not a library-specific or cataloging-specific tool and can be used to analyze all kinds of data, be it government datasets, bibliographic information, circulation statistics, etc. This application in some respects functions as a spreadsheet on steroids and can easily process hundreds of thousands of records at a time. Some of its helpful features include faceted searching and editing of a dataset, a comprehensive revision history and ability to undo commands in an instant, and built-in connections to many publicly-available databases.

Microsoft Excel

Excel is that trusty spreadsheet program that's been lurking on librarians' computers since the dawn of time. It is an essential tool for any librarian to be familiar with, especially CMLs working with large datasets. Excel can be used to view, sort, analyze, and edit bibliographic, licensing, acquisitions, and other data. One common use is to extract a set of records from a library management system, download it to Excel, edit it, and then overlay the edited records back into the system. Excel's capabilities overlap with MarcEdit and OpenRefine to a certain extent, though being a general use application does not have the deep library-specific functions that are found in those other applications.

ExifTool

ExifTool is another free program designed for editing metadata, but in this case the meta information is associated with digital images and other audiovisual files (www.sno.phy.queensu.ca/~phil/exiftool/). ExifTool was created in 2003 by software developer Phil Harvey and remains free to use as a Perl-based command line module or a downloadable GUI program. This program can extract and edit the metadata embedded in digital images and can also be used to add additional metadata that the cataloging librarian may wish to include in the files. Originally, ExifTool was designed to work with metadata tags in the Exchangeable Image File Format (EXIF) but now it can read and manipulate metadata from other schemas and the makernotes embedded into images by digital cameras. This program is an extremely capable tool for CMLs who routinely work with digital images and A/V files.

Metadata++

Metadata++ is a lightweight metadata explorer built for the Windows environment. In appearance and navigation this program would look familiar to a librarian used to using Windows Explorer. Metadata++

can display metadata for almost any file but is especially helpful for unearthing and editing meta information associated with audio, video and image formats. Whereas ExifTool was designed to focus more on images, Metadata++ has a broader focus on media files generally. Use the program to explore, edit, add, or delete metadata from your chosen files. You can export metadata to a variety of formats, including TXT, XML, HTML, and JSON and can append information in the form of a sidecar to files that normally wouldn't have metadata. This program is developed by Logipole and is freely downloadable (www.logipole.com/metadata++-en.htm).

Oxygen XML Editor

Oxygen XML is a product of the Syncro Soft company and offers a full suite of capabilities for working with XML documents. Their flagship product allows you to create, edit, collaborate, and publish various types of XML documents, including schemas, CSS, and XSLT. The XML editor has a built-in validation tool that will help ensure your XML remains well-formed as you author or edit documents. Oxygen XML also allows you to publish your document in various outputs, including PDF, ePUB, or HTML. Although this product is not free, Syncro Soft offers discounted academic and personal pricing that could make it an affordable option for metadata librarians (www.oxygenxml.com).

Resource Management and Discovery Systems

It is vital for any CML to be familiar with the product documentation associated with their resource management and discovery systems. This documentation typically describes the various workflow functionalities one may encounter while using the system. Locate this documentation as soon as possible and familiarize yourself with the sections related to cataloging, importing records, and processing materials. The quality of system documentation varies by vendor and system, but when used in tandem with the user group listservs referenced below, you will likely have enough at your disposal to perform the work of a sudden CML.

Discussed in more detail in Chapter 1, here are some examples of various resource management and discovery systems:

ILSs/OPACs: Innovative's Millennium, Ex Libris' Voyager, Ex Libris' Aleph, SirsiDynix's Symphony, SirsiDynix's Horizon, Koha, and Evergreen.

LSPs: Innovative's Polaris, Ex Libris' Alma, Innovative's Sierra, OCLC's WMS, SirsiDynix's BlueCloud, and FOLIO (still in development as of this publication).

Repositories: OCLC's CONTENTdm, Elsevier's (bepress) Digital Commons, DSpace, Samvera, Fedora, Islandora, and Omeka.

Discovery layers: Ex Libris' Primo, ProQuest's Summon, EBSCO's EDS, OCLC's Worldshare, VuFind, and Blacklight.

Marshall Breeding's annual Library Systems report is a very informative reference point into which types of libraries (academic, public, special, etc.) are using which systems, including how many have migrated away from their legacy systems.[32]

Ongoing Community Engagement and Professional Development

Staying in touch with the cataloging and metadata communities in addition to continuing education are essential to any CML. Not only are the cataloging and metadata frameworks, standards, and schemas in constant flux, so too are the tools that we use to manage and manipulate descriptive data. As different versions and iterations of these components get tested, released, and implemented, CMLs are asked to stay on top of these developments. A healthy mix of joining professional organizations, following listservs, attending conferences, and participating in development opportunities help CMLs stay current.

Professional Organizations

Many CMLs belong to professional organizations to offer financial support to and participate in ongoing initiatives important to our communities. While there is a very real possibility your institution will not let you volunteer your time or reimburse you for membership fees, do not let these inconveniences deter you from participating in some form or another. There are a number of benefits one can enjoy from joining professional organizations.

First and foremost, these groups act as lobbyists on behalf of their members for important issues like government funding and policies. In our experience, librarians tend to be quite engaged in the political process, and supporting the professional organizations that represent our interests is not taken lightly. For example, it is common practice to list membership affiliations on one's CV to show a vested interest as a community member.

Another benefit is the opportunity to serve on various projects and initiatives, which is a great way to network, learn from colleagues, assist in research, and play an administrative role in an organization. Since everyone is short on time, service to professional organizations is greatly appreciated and looked upon favorably. This is also true for regional subchapters or state-based organizations.

Finally, these bodies help produce and review the various standards and schemas we work with on a daily basis. They offer clear avenues to direct questions, comments, or concerns. Ensuring that individuals with the appropriate qualifications and skill sets drive this important work forward is critical to the success of CMLs everywhere.

Some important organizations that sudden CMLs should consider joining are:

> **ACRL**—Association of College & Research Libraries
>
> **ALA**—American Library Association
>
> **ALCTS**—Association for Library Collections & Technical Services
>
> **LITA**—Library Information Technology Association
>
> **MOUG**—Music OCLC Users Group
>
> **NASIG**—North American Serials Interest Group
>
> **OLAC**—Online Audiovisual Catalogers

Relevant Listservs

Listservs are one of the most useful tools CMLs rely on to ask peers questions and seek advice. While correspondence can be too voluminous to check daily or even weekly, it's important to monitor the listservs you deem relevant to your daily responsibilities to stay abreast of issues and developments. A common way to control the flow of information is to create a separate inbox folder for each listserv and use filtering rules to automatically sort listserv emails. Without such a filtering system, it may be difficult to parse important emails requiring your immediate attention.

Many listservs have general policies about posting etiquette, which are typically listed on the listserv's homepage. To illustrate, advertisements or solicitations from vendors are not allowed on certain listservs but encouraged on others. Some also have a statement about respectfulness and inclusivity, as well as a mechanism to police bad behavior. Additionally, each listserv has some underlying rules of engagement that will become clearer by following it over time. For example, some listservs tend to be more contentious by nature, whereas others are more collaborative and practical. In our experience, contentious behavior typically revolves around copyright interpretation. In general, please make sure you are mindful of these dynamics when posting questions or comments to the various listservs you become a part of.

Some notable listservs in the cataloging community include:

CATALOGING AND METADATA LISTSERVS

Program for Cooperative Cataloging (PCC) listserv (PCCLIST@LISTSERV.LOC.GOV)

BIBCO listserv (BIBCO@LISTSERV.LOC.GOV)

CONSER listserv (CONSRLST@LISTSERV.LOC.GOV)

SACO listserv (SACOLIST@LISTSERV.LOC.GOV)

ALCTS listservs (http://lists.ala.org/sympa/lists/divisions/alcts)

Autocat listserv (AUTOCAT@LISTSERV.SYR.EDU)

ACRL Technical Services Interest Group (acr-igts@lists.ala.org)

Metadata Librarians
(MDL, metadatalibrarians@lists.monarchos.com)

Metadata Standards (metastand@lists.ala.org)

BIBFRAME (BIBFRAME@LISTSERV.LOC.GOV)

RDA (http://lists.ala.org/sympa/info/rda-l)

EAD (EAD@LISTSERV.LOC.GOV)

MARC (MARC@LISTSERV.LOC.GOV)

METS (METS@LISTSERV.LOC.GOV)

SERIALST (LISTSERV@listserv.nasig.org)

MAP-L (MAPS-L@LISTSERV.UGA.EDU)

Music Library Association listserv
(MLA-L, mla-l-subscribe@indiana.edu)

VideoLib (videolib@lists.berkeley.edu)

eduCAT (EDUCAT@LISTSERV.LOC.GOV)

DCGeneral (DC-GENERAL@JISCMAIL.AC.UK)

OLAC-L (olac-l@oclclists.org)

MOUG-L (moug-l@oclclistsorg)

RBMS-L (http://rbms.info/publications/discussion_list)

Library System User Community Listservs

There are also listservs dedicated to specific management systems and discovery layers. These listservs are great places to learn about known issues, hear about performance issues, ask general questions about functionality or implementing a new service, and so on. Generally speaking, the communities are quite active and willing to share their expertise. We'd recommend signing up for whatever products are being used by your library and tracking the discussion for a while to determine whether you find it useful. These lists should be relatively easy to locate by searching online. Examples of such listservs include:

Ex Libris maintains listservs for each of their products
(https://exlibrisusers.org/listinfo)

Innovative User Group (INNOPAC) (http://innovativeusers
.org/iug-forum/innopac-archives.html)

SirsiDynix (COSUGI)
(www.cosugi.org/listserv-subscriptions)

Koha Listservs
(https://koha-community.org/support/koha-mailing-lists)

ProQuest Summon Listserv (summonclients@lists.summon
.serialssolutions.com)

VuFind Listservs (https://sourceforge.net/p/vufind/
mailman/message/35680602)

Fedora Listservs (https://lists.fedoraproject.org/archives)

Islandora Listservs
(http://islandora.ca/content/welcome-islandora-listserv)

Samvera Google Groups (https://groups.google.com/
forum/#!forum/samvera-tech and https://groups.google
.com/forum/#!forum/samvera-community)

Other Noteworthy Listservs

COLLIB (COLLIB-L@lists.ala.org)

PUBLIB (PUBLIB@LISTSERV.OCLCLISTS.ORG)

FEDLIB (FEDLIB@LISTSERV.LOC.GOV)

ERIL (ERIL-L@LISTSERV.BINGHAMTON.EDU)

LibLicense (liblicense-l@listserv.crl.edu)

Web4Lib (web4lib@listserv.uc.edu)

Code4Lib (CODE4LIB@LISTS.CLIR.ORG)

GIS4Lib (gis4lib@u.washington.edu)

ALA (http://lists.ala.org/sympa/lists)

Noteworthy Conferences

Attending conferences is a great avenue for professional development
and networking. And even if you can't attend, it's worth reviewing

programming, seeing if there is a live streaming option, taking part in Twitter conversations, and trying to obtain presentation materials that are often distributed afterward. Here are some important conferences to be aware of:

> ALA Midwinter Meeting and Annual Conference
>
> Association for Information Science and Technology (ASIS&T) Research Data Access & Preservation (RDAP) Summit
>
> ALCTS programs at Midwinter Meeting and Annual Conference
>
> ACRL conferences
>
> Charleston Conference: Issues in Book and Serial Acquisition
>
> Coalition for Networked Information (CNI) Biannual Membership Meetings
>
> Code4Lib Annual Conference
>
> Computers in Libraries Annual Conference
>
> Digital Library Federation (DLF) Forum
>
> Electronic Resources & Libraries (ER&L) Conference
>
> International Federation of Library Associations and Institutions (IFLA) World Library and Information Congress
>
> LITA Forum
>
> Metadata and Semantics Research (MTSR) Conference
>
> Music OCLC Users Group (MOUG) Meeting
>
> NASIG Annual Conference
>
> National Digital Stewardship Alliance (NDSA) Digital Preservation Conference
>
> NISO Virtual Conferences
>
> Online Audiovisual Catalogers (OLAC) Biennial Conference

Open Repositories (OR)

Society of American Archivists (SSA) Annual Meeting

Further, there are a plethora of regional, state, and vendor-specific conferences that are equally worthwhile to monitor, attend, and submit proposals to. It is often easier to network at these events since they tend to be smaller and there's a more immediate connection between attendees and the programming.

Continuing Education Opportunities

Continuing education is a very important part of CML's ongoing responsibilities, but is often neglected due to the demands of our jobs. The variety of frameworks, standards, schemas, vocabularies, systems, and other tools we work with are often in flux, where one ripple can have far ranging effects through the entire resource description ecosystem we rely upon. Since a lot of the tools and resources we use are near the forefront of certain technological curves, there always seems to be a mix of components that are being phased out, re-envisioned, or newly deployed. There are simply too many developments happening simultaneously for any one CML to keep track of, let alone understand how these changes will affect our daily responsibilities over time.

While professional organizations, listservs, and conferences will help keep you informed and offer practical examples for tackling problems, continuing education opportunities (webinars, workshops, training sessions, classes, etc.) are often better at teaching new concepts, providing in-depth explanations of potential changes, and demonstrating new use cases. Luckily, you should not need to actively seek out continuing education opportunities if you cast a broad net when participating in professional organizations, listservs, and conferences. A wide range of continuing education opportunities are constantly advertised in these forums, some of which require a fee and others that are free.

Typically, the most expensive opportunities come in the form of in-person instruction, whether as intensive courses or pre/post-conference sessions. Webinars tend to be more moderately priced, if there is a fee associated at all. Since not everyone has access to continuing educations funds, we've put together a short list of free materials that are continual sources of training materials:

> Library of Congress Catalogers Learning Workshop
> (www.loc.gov/catworkshop)

> Library of Congress Webcasts
> (www.loc.gov/today/cyberlc/index.php)

> ALCTS Continuing Education YouTube channel
> (www.youtube.com/user/alctsce)

> ALCTS monthly e-Forums
> (www.ala.org/alcts/confevents/upcoming/e-forum)

> ALA Webinar Archive
> (www.ala.org/alcts/confevents/past/webinar)

SUMMARY

While the above represents our attempt at a concise summary of the tools of the trade we generally rely on, it is by no means exhaustive. There are diverse resources and tools available that facilitate the description process and the metadata manipulation often associated with it. Given the expansive way in which information can be transmitted and subsequently described for discovery purposes, there will never be a CML fluent with every resource and tool that is available to the larger community.

The information discussed above and in the previous chapters should provide any sudden CML the necessary foundations to tackle their new responsibilities. As you move forward and begin to participate in the cooperative description process happening globally, please remember that you do not always have to operate in isolation and reinvent the wheel. You have access to colleagues of varying skill sets and specializations that have accumulated collective wisdom far greater than any one individual is capable of achieving.

NOTES

1. Barbara Tillett, What is FRBR?: A Conceptual Model for the Bibliographic Universe, 2004, www.loc.gov/cds/downloads/FRBR.PDF.

2. Functional Requirements for Bibliographic Records, Final Report, IFLA Study Group on the Functional Requirements for Bibliographic Records. – München: K.G. Saur, 1998. (UBCIM Publications, New Series ; v. 19).

3. W3C, RDF 1.1 Concepts and Abstract Syntax, 2014, www.w3.org/TR/2014/REC-rdf11-concepts-20140225/#section-Introduction.

4. CIDOC, Conceptual Reference Model, www.cidoc-crm.org.

5. RDA Toolkit (Chicago: American Library Association; Ottawa: Canadian Library Association; London: Chartered Institute of Library and Information Professionals [CILIP], 2010–), www.rdatoolkit.org.

6. Society of American Archivists, Describing Archives: A Content Standard (DACS), Second Edition, www2.archivists.org/groups/technical-subcommittee-on-describing-archives-a-content-standard-dacs/dacs.

7. Library of Congress, PREMIS, www.loc.gov/standards/premis/index.html

8. Library of Congress, MARC Standards Frequently Asked Questions, www.loc.gov/marc/faq.html#definition.

9. Library of Congress, METS: Metadata Encoding & Transmission Standard, www.loc.gov/standards/mets.

10. Library of Congress, MODS: Metadata Object Description Schema, www.loc.gov/standards/mods/mods-overview.html.

11. www.loc.gov/ead/eaddev.html.

12. Staatsbibliothek zu Berlin, <EAC-CPF>, http://eac.staatsbibliothek-berlin.de/index.php?id=61

13. Introducing schema.org: Search engines come together for a richer web. (https://googleblog.blogspot.com/2011/06/introducing-schemaorg-search-engines.html) 2 June 2011.

14. U.S. National Library of Medicine, Medical Subject Headings, www.nlm.nih.gov/mesh/meshhome.html.

15. J. Paul Getty Trust, Art & Architecture Thesaurus Online, www.getty.edu/research/tools/vocabularies/aat/about.html.

16. OCLC, Connexion, www.oclc.org/en/connexion.html.

17. OCLC, Bibliographic Formats and Standards, www.oclc.org/bibformats/en.html.

18. Oliver, Chris. "Introducing RDA: A Guide to the Basics," (Chicago: American Library Association, 2010), www.npc.edu/sites/files/shared/library/Introducing%20RDA.pdf.

19. Ibid.

20. RDA Toolkit, 3R Project Status Report #3, www.rdatoolkit.org/3Rproject/ SR3.

21. Library of Congress, Cataloger's Desktop Subscription Pricing, www.loc .gov/cds/desktop/prices.html.

22. Library of Congress, Classification Web – Orders & Pricing, www.loc.gov/ cds/classweb/classweborder.html.

23. ArchivesSpace, Mission & Guiding Principles, https://archivesspace.org/ about/mission.

24. Library of Congress, About the PCC, www.loc.gov/aba/pcc/about.

25. Program for Cooperative Cataloging (PCC) Provider-Neutral E-Resource MARC Record Guidelines, www.loc.gov/aba/pcc/scs/documents/PCC-PN -guidelines.html.

26. Program for Cooperative Cataloging, BIBCO Standard Record (BSR): RDA Metadata Application Profile, 2017, www.loc.gov/aba/pcc/bibco/ documents/PCC-RDA-BSR.pdf.

27. Program for Cooperative Cataloging, BIBCO Participants' Manual, 2014, www.loc.gov/aba/pcc/bibco/documents/bpm.pdf.

28. Program for Cooperative Cataloging, Integrating Resources: A Cataloging Manual, 2015, www.loc.gov/aba/pcc/conser/word/Module35.doc.

29. Program for Cooperative Cataloging, CONSER Documentation and Updates, www.loc.gov/aba/pcc/conser/more-documentation.html.

30. Terry Reese, About MarcEdit, http://marcedit.reeset.net/about-marcedit

31. OpenRefine History, 2013, http://openrefine.org/my%20category/2013/ 10/12/openrefine-history.html.

32. Marshall Breeding, Library Systems Report 2017, https://american librariesmagazine.org/2017/05/01/library-systems-report-2017.

CHAPTER SEVEN

Conclusion
The Future of Cataloging and Metadata

As detailed throughout Chapters 2 and 4, CMLs are currently anticipating an enormous shift in their daily practice once linked data architectures are widely implemented across the web.

The hope is that linked data implementation will move our descriptions of library resources out of their various silos, and library metadata will be visible on and native to the open web—available to search engines and future web applications in ways we can't even fully envision yet, but which would increase accessibility and bring much-needed exposure to valuable LAM resources. For our institutions to remain relevant, our resources must have more of a presence in the digital world than they do now. We have been behind the curve since the 1990s; now is our chance to make up ground. Early adoption of linked data technologies may put us *ahead* of the curve, for once. When the web completes its next evolution, let us hope library data is already there, rich and curated and powerful, awaiting new uses by machines and by people.

However, implementing such a fundamental shift in our daily operations will involve a great deal of our time and resources. For instance, development of new standards and revisions of existing practice needed to support this future environment has already involved years of effort by various groups in the CML professional community, and that work is still underway. As of early 2018, BIBFRAME 2.0 was still being tested by Library of Congress catalogers, the Library Reference Model (LRM) framework had just been finalized and adopted, and the entire structure and content of RDA was in the process of revision.

When we are finally ready to distribute and implement new standards and best practices, more challenges await. Vendors or libraries themselves must develop an entirely new generation of automated library systems before our library linked data can be properly stored, indexed, searched, and displayed in public interfaces. All CMLs and paraprofessional staff will need to undergo training in these new standards and systems. Institutions with fewer resources will have more difficulty adopting such changes, and will need to depend heavily on their vendors, larger peer institutions, and guiding bodies like the PCC and OCLC for the tools to move forward.

Luckily, the general trend at the moment is that the relevant players above understand the context of the ecosystem they work within and realize that interoperability is key to their future viability. Accordingly, there is active collaboration happening across the industry and many are willing to play nicely together to achieve better results for all. As information providers make it easier to share and synchronize their metadata with other collection management systems, there should be less need to create metadata from scratch but a greater need for the cataloging and metadata community to figure out how it wants to review, modify, and enhance vendor records for the collective's consumption. That being said, the quality and consistency of vendor records remains problematic. Information providers and the metadata and cataloging community must find ways to advance this issue in order to reduce duplication and free up resources for other initiatives.

FUTURE ENVIRONMENTS

Although the cooperative cataloging network has radically improved the kind of resource description libraries can offer their patrons, there is still much that can be improved in terms of making our collections more visible, more accessible, and more connected with the web.

Using the cooperative foundation we have built in the twentieth century, cataloging and metadata professionals are now looking forward to the next evolution of web-based information, the Semantic Web, which we hope to use to harmonize our data with web standards and bring our resources out of their silos. To understand exactly how this will work, we need to briefly explore current and expected web technologies, and also discuss planned standards that CMLs have not yet implemented on any wide scale. Because this section looks into a still uncertain future, you may wish to review Chapters 3 and 4 first to get a handle on standards used in current practice, and return to this section to learn how those standards are preparing us for a leap into a new cataloging and metadata paradigm.

When the web was initially created, it was comprised of a collection of documents marked up with machine-readable tags. Those tags instructed machines on how to render information online for humans to read. The HTML tag **<p>**, for instance, has to do with formatting. A web browser reading **<p> Zora Neale Hurston wrote *Their Eyes Were Watching God*</p>** only knows that the text should be rendered as a separate paragraph on the screen. The machine has no idea *what kind* of information the text is conveying.

Of course the web has come a long way since its creation, and a lot of information expressed on the web is much more structured and interlinked than it used to be. Metadata is what drives this interconnection. Consider the way Netflix can suggest things like "TV Shows with a Strong Female Lead," or Spotify can recommend new artists to you. Those companies have developed metadata tags that help machines not only relay content, but understand what *kind* of content is being described and trace connections between descriptions.

But these examples involve proprietary metadata schemas, which aren't relevant to libraries. In our field, we need an *open* web standard that allows us to mark up our resource descriptions in meaningful ways so that web browsers and applications can actually understand what's in our collections. Right now, our resource descriptions are viewable online only because our ILS software can generate HTML versions of MARC records from our local databases. So patrons can to an extent search and view our resource descriptions (if they suspend their normal web-searching behaviors and learn instead to navigate specialized library interfaces), but that information is not what we call *machine-actionable* in any useful way, and it's not truly web native. As mentioned previously, the open web standard Resource Description Framework (RDF) is poised to change that.

The word "semantic" in the term Semantic Web refers to a web of information encoded in a way that permits machines to draw actual semantic meaning from the code they read, instead of just acting as passive relay agents. This is accomplished through RDF's triple structure, which identifies each little byte of information and connects those bytes together. For instance, if we make the statement **<subject: *Their Eyes Were Watching God*> <predicate: written by> <object: Zora Neale Hurston>**, we're beginning to help the computer understand what is being expressed. Of course the computer needs additional context for understanding who Zora Neale Hurston is, what the "writer of" relationship means, and that *Their Eyes Were Watching God* is a creative work. In other words, we need to create dictionaries for the computer to consult—i.e., collections of standard identifiers for all the entities and relationships we're trying to describe.

This is the concept behind linked data. To help machines understand triple statements, we need to establish a unique identifier for every person, place, concept, type of resource, etc. that we reference. These collections of Uniform Resource Identifiers, or URIs, serve as dictionaries for machine reference and learning, and also are a means for easily disambiguating names and titles and concepts. The term "linked data" often gets used in a broader sense as well, as a reference to the interlinked environment and Semantic Web practices that URI usage is expected to bring about.

Ontologies are another tool that further assist the machine in understanding exactly what is being expressed in an RDF triple statement. All librarians are already familiar with the concept of ontologies, though perhaps not by that name. Library of Congress

Classification is a sort of ontology, because it organizes information into certain categories and then arranges those categories in relation to each other. The field of ontology is an ancient one, and in the classic definition it simply means a philosophical modeling of a particular domain of knowledge—as discussed earlier, a mapping out of the universe in question. In the web context, however, an ontology has a more technical and specific function, and refers to a set of vocabulary terms with a standardized structure that defines classes of things (or entities) and properties of (or relationships between) those classes. As mentioned previously, RDF is a very high-level data model; an ontology is a set of terms that can be used to actually *make* RDF statements. If RDF is the grammar, ontologies are the vocabulary we use to construct grammatical sentences.

To put it all together, RDF gives us the basic triple structure for making a statement. An ontology defines certain entities and their properties, and gives us specific vocabulary terms to use in that statement. Finally, URIs provide computers with definitions for all the terms used. See the table below for a visual diagram of these interacting layers.

(4) URI references	URI from the LC NAF for Their Eyes Were Watching God http://id.loc.gov/authorities/names/no2009056334	URI from the BIBFRAME ontology for property "agent" http://id.loc.gov/ontologies/bibframe.html#p_agent	URI from Virtual International Authority File (VIAF) for Zora Neale Hurston http://viaf.org/viaf/62824341/
(3) BIBFRAME ontology terms	bf:Work	bf:agent	bf:Person
(2) underlying ontology elements	Class	[has]property	Class
(1) underlying RDF elements	Subject	predicate	Object
	entity →	*relationship →*	*entity*

Lines 1 and 2 illustrate the abstract structure of a triple statement being used to say something with ontology terms; we can see how this structure hearkens back to the entity/relationship pattern we discussed at length in the beginning of the chapter.

The example terms (or "labels") used in line 3 are drawn from BIBFRAME 2.0, the latest version of the ontology developed by Library of Congress for RDF-based description of library resources. Note in line 4 of the illustration that the URIs have all been drawn from different sources, and this is again by design. RDF statements can refer to any URI regardless of its creator or its location on the web, which gives us great flexibility in our description.

Currently, we expect BIBFRAME to succeed MARC21 as the means by which we mark up, index, exchange, and display our traditional cataloging data. But catalog records are not the only resource descriptions currently siloed inside library interfaces. Resource descriptions rendered in metadata schemas like Dublin Core or Encoded Archival Description (EAD) are still trapped in their own separate repositories, usually searchable and discoverable only if patrons navigate to a special library interface, or to larger public databases like the Digital Public Library of America (DPLA). But in the envisioned linked data future, such descriptions would also be expressed in RDF, using their own web ontology terms. For example, the Metadata Authority Description Schema (MADS) already has an RDF-compliant ontology established and available online,[1] as do a number of other metadata schemas preparing for the next evolution of the web.

Right now, along with other web information communities, libraries are still in the development stage of this new future: creating new ontologies like BIBFRAME, establishing ontologies for existing schema, publishing vast repositories of URIs, and holding conversations about linked data principles and best practices. Systems that can store, index, and display triple data are still being built, and are not widely in use, either in the library world or on the commercial web. But once the infrastructure exists to broadly implement the technologies of the Semantic Web, and once web browsers and applications are able to read, interpret, and manipulate linked data, it won't matter if library resource descriptions use terms from a number of different ontologies or URIs from hundreds of different sources. All web ontologies have a uniform structure that machines will be able to navigate. All URIs have certain standard qualities. So for instance, if BIBFRAME lacks a term for a particular concept a CML needs to express, it would be perfectly acceptable to use a term from the MADS ontology instead, and reference the URI for that term. The adaptability of this method of describing resources is an exciting prospect.

So what does this all mean for the nitty-gritty work of cataloging and metadata? Ultimately, CMLs will need to become familiar with the different ontologies that may emerge and become authorized for description of resources. Because their work often consists of creating and transforming metadata on a large scale, metadata librarians will need to know the inner workings of those ontologies and other technical aspects of related web standards. Catalogers, however, will be able to devote less of their headspace to the coding happening behind the scenes, which is a big change; for decades, cataloging librarians have had to maintain a detailed grasp of MARC tags, indicators, subfields, and so on. Instead, after the transition to a linked data environment, catalogers will be free to focus on the intellectual considerations of resource description (What subjects do I assign to this resource? How do I reflect this person's relationship to the resource?) and devote more time to establishing the identities of people, places, and concepts. This will be crucial because URIs must exist for any referenced concept for the Semantic Web to be as powerful as we envision. It is expected that institutions like OCLC and the PCC will still play a role in guiding the creation of this kind of shared, authoritative library data, but new CMLs should also anticipate some entirely novel protocols will emerge.

It is important to provide a note about the description of people and places going forward, as we anticipate a sharp increase in the amount of identity management work that CMLs will be called upon to handle. Although neutrality is a much-referenced tenet of good cataloging and metadata practice, it's important to recognize that true neutrality is not realistic. CMLs as private individuals come to their work with a built-in set of implicit biases and gaps in knowledge, and the same is true of the institutions and systems through which we produce our work. As Dr. Hope Olson's seminal 2002 book on the subject points out, the work of naming things involves a power dynamic that it is irresponsible to ignore. New CMLs can engage more with these ethical questions by participating in such conversations as #critcat, and attending the growing number of professional workshops and formal discussions about equity, diversity, and inclusion in cataloging and metadata practice.

Advocating for the Profession

The next five to ten years in cataloging and metadata work will be crucial to the continued survival of LAM institutions everywhere. How can we ensure that our administrators and our colleagues in other fields of LAM work are tuned into the importance of this work?

First and foremost, we must promote the understanding that cataloging and metadata creation is a public service, just like reference or instruction or community programs. As Antonio Panizzi argued long ago, when British Museum administrators criticized his Ninety-One Cataloguing Rules as overly detailed and time-consuming to implement, describing resources is about more than inventory control. The work is meaningless unless it leads patrons on a journey of discovery, empowering them to explore our resources via endless connected pathways. Our collections are vast and complicated, and our public services colleagues can only ever hope to provide personal guidance to a small percentage of our users. More and more, our online search interfaces will serve as the only points of interaction between some patrons and their local libraries.

Thus, as pointed out in Chapter 1, even though we mostly work behind the scenes, we are still communicating directly with our users through our resource descriptions. Having the proper tools, the right training, appropriate systems, and connections to our peers in the field are essential to producing quality work. Ask your administrators, what kind of damage does library credibility suffer each time a patron faces obstacles to online discovery? A robust and well-supported cataloging and metadata staff, working in cooperation with any web services, accessibility, and/or usability staff, can make sure online discovery is a positive experience for each and every user.

Of course, CMLs in academic institutions have little to no control over the usability of any third-party subscription databases such as those provided by EBSCO or ProQuest. But as unified search tools like discovery layers incorporate this third-party content more and more, input from CMLs about metadata characteristics and behavior is still key.

Cataloger as Manager and Advocate

As we described above, what we catalog is evolving away from the traditional printed book which, in turn, is forcing the library and CML to evolve as well. You can see this specifically in how organizational charts are morphing to digitization, job ads are adding metadata to duties assigned, and not every cataloger who retires is replaced. It sounds discouraging but it is nothing new to those who work in tech services: change is constant and CMLs adapt to stay relevant because our users need our work to ensure their research is consistent and our materials stay discoverable.

One major change is that local and unique collections are more and more requested for use. Catalogers can increase accessibility by learning more about local history, prominent figures, etc. This aids in highlighting the uniqueness of the collection, representing minority populations, and more.

What can a CML do when cataloging hours are reduced or positions are not filled/replaced? You emphasize the importance of what you do. If you can, you get numbers to support this: circulation statistics are your friends. For example, the newest best seller has X amount of checkouts and you have twenty books from the same author waiting to be cataloged. You have the data to say that spending time cataloging those other titles will benefit your user. This applies to all titles waiting to be cataloged. Find the relationship between what's in your backlog with what is being used in your library.

Succession Planning

We touched briefly on cataloging not receiving consistent time and resources. How do you save time and resources when you need to train a new cataloger? If you were stuck doing this, more than likely, someone else will have to follow in your footsteps. To ensure continuity between employees as well as consistency over records, you or your supervisor will have to plan for the transition. This is called succession planning and is defined as the planned preparation for an employee's departure from a department or institution, whether from resignation or retirement. William H. Weare, Jr. described it further in his article as "a process generally used to identify, train, and prepare select employees to fill key leadership roles within the company . . . succession planning can be a part of a broader strategy to provide continuity, ease executive transitions, and perpetuate the organization." The goal is to ease the transition with as few disruptions to job duties as possible. The larger benefit is identifying employee strengths and cultivating talents from within the organization. Hall-Ellis and Grealy state

> Succession planning allows an organization to anticipate new leadership, assess the skills and knowledge of employees, identify individuals who have leadership potential, and provide professional development opportunities, mentoring, and experiences to prepare the library staff for personnel changes.

We've gone over why, so now let's talk about how to create a smooth transition. Most importantly, create documentation. Documentation can be written in multiple ways: essays to describe details as well as how duties impact large picture objectives; checklists which guide the reader step-by-step through a workflow; and more. Follow formats laid out in other documents written in your organization. Be sure to make it easy for someone in a hurry or at the beginning of their learning curve to follow.

CONCLUSION

We hope that in your review of this book, you have learned some of the information that you will need to be a successful Cataloging and Metadata Librarian. While the vast amount of information that CMLs use on a daily basis can be daunting at first, reviewing the resources and information presented here will help you to learn many of the standards, tools, and resources that CMLs use on a regular basis in order to provide access to all that is available at the library.

REFERENCES

Hall-Ellis, Sylvia D., and Deborah S. Grealy. "The Dreyfus Model of Skill Acquisition: A Career Development Framework for Succession Planning and Management in Academic Libraries." *College & Research Libraries*, vol. 74, no. 6, Jan. 2013, pp. 587–603., doi:10.5860/crl12-349.

Galbraith, Quinn, et al. "A case for succession planning." *Library Management*, vol. 33, no. 4/5, Nov. 2012, pp. 221–240., doi:10.1108/01435121211242272.

Weare, William H. "Succession Planning in Academic Libraries: A Reconsideration." *Advances in Library Administration and Organization Library Staffing for the Future*, 2015, pp. 313–361., doi:10.1108/s0732 -067120150000034013.

NOTE

1. Library of Congress, MADS/RDF Primer, 2015, www.loc.gov/standards/ mads/rdf.

Common Acronyms Used by Cataloging and Metadata Librarians

AACR – Anglo-American Cataloging Rules

AACR2 – Anglo-American Cataloging Rules, 2nd edition

AAT – Getty's Art & Architecture Thesaurus

ACRL – Association of College & Research Libraries

ALCTS – Association for Library Collections & Technical Services

AP – Access Point

API – Application programming interface

ARL – Association of Research Libraries

BIBCO – Bibliographic Cooperative

BIBFRAME – Bibliographic Framework

CCO – Cataloging Cultural Objects

CIDOC – International Committee for Documentation

CML – Cataloging and Metadata Librarian

CONA – Getty's Cultural Objects Name Authority

CONSER – Cooperative Online Serials Program

CRM – Conceptual Reference Model

CSV – Comma-separated values

DACS – Describing Archives: A Content Standard

DC – Dublin Core

DCMI – Dublin Core Metadata Initiative

DCRM – Descriptive Cataloging of Rare Materials

DDC – Dewey Decimal Classification

DLF – Digital Library Federation

DPLA – Digital Public Library of America

EAD – Encoded Archival Description

FRAD – Functional Requirements for Authority Data

FRBR – Functional Requirements for Bibliographic Records

FRSAD – Functional Requirements for Subject Authority Data

GNIS – Geographic Names Information System

HTML – Hypertext Markup Language

IFLA – International Federation of Library Associations and Institutions

ISBD – International Standard Bibliographic Description

JSON-LD – JavaScript Object Notation for Linked Data

LAM – Libraries, archives and museums

LC – Library of Congress

LCC – Library of Congress Classification

LCGFT – Library of Congress Genre/Form Terms

LCSH – Library of Congress Subject Headings

LITA – Library and Information Technology Association

LRM – Library Reference Model

LSP – Library Services Platform

MADS – Metadata Authority Description Schema

MARC – Machine-Readable Cataloging

MeSH – Medical Subject Headings

METS – Metadata Encoding and Transcription Standard

MIX – Metadata for Images in XML Standard

MLA-BCC – Music Library Association's Bibliographic Control Committee

MODS – Metadata Object Description Schema

N3 – Notation 3

NACO – Name Authority Cooperative Program

NAF – Library of Congress Name Authority File

OAI-PMH – Open Archives Initiative Protocol for Metadata Harvesting

OLAC – Online Audiovisual Catalogers

OPAC – Online Public Access Catalog

PCC – Program for Cooperative Cataloging

PDF – Portable Document Format

PREMIS – Preservation Metadata: Implementation Strategies

RDA – Resource Description and Access

RDF – Resource Description Framework

RDFS – Resource Description Framework Schema

SACO – Subject Authority Cooperative Program

SHM – Subject Headings Manual

TEI – Text Encoding Initiative

TGM – Thesaurus for Graphic Materials

TGN – Getty's Thesaurus of Geographic Names

Turtle – Terse RDF Triple Language

ULAN – Getty's Union List of Artist Names

URI – Uniform Resource Identifier

W3C – World Wide Web Consortium

XML – Extensible Markup Language

XSLT – Extensible Stylesheet Language

About the Editors and Contributors

EDITOR and CONTRIBUTOR

JEREMY MYNTTI (MLIS, University of Alabama, 2011) is Head of Digital Library Services at the University of Utah's J. Willard Marriott Library. Prior to this position, he was Head of Cataloging and Metadata Services and the ILS administrator for the University of Utah Libraries. He began his cataloging career in 2003 at a library services vendor.

SERIES EDITOR

SUSAN THOMAS currently serves as the ALCTS Monographs Editor. She is also the Director of Collection Services for the Schurz Library and Subject Librarian for the Health Sciences at Indiana University South Bend. Susan has 27 years of experience working in academic libraries. Prior to her current position at IU South Bend, Susan served as the Facilitator for Reference Services and Archivist (1995-1997) at Valdosta State University (Georgia), the Assistant Head of the Regents Center Library and Bibliographer for Social Welfare at the University of Kansas/Edwards Campus, and as a Medical Reference Librarian at the University of Oklahoma Health Sciences Center Library. Susan holds a B.A. in Psychology (Indiana University), a Master's in Library and Information Science (Indiana University), and a Master's in Public Affairs (Indiana University South Bend).

BEN ABRAHAMSE (MLIS, McGill University, 2008) is Cataloging Coordinator at the MIT Libraries. His professional interests include the cataloging of serials, special collections, and conference publications.

WHITNEY BUCCICONE (MLS, Indiana University, 2006; MA in Arts Administration, Indiana University, 2016) is the Special Collections Cataloging Librarian for the University of Washington Libraries. From 2006 to 2016, she held multiple paraprofessional cataloging positions at the Lilly Library, Indiana University Bloomington, before beginning her position at UW. Current interests include cataloging, special collections, digital collections, management, and backlog elimination.

STEPHEN BUSS (MLS, University of Maryland, 2013) currently serves as Systems and Reference Librarian at University of the Sciences in Philadelphia. He began his library career as Reference & Emerging Technologies Librarian at USciences following six years in the content department at a small, independent publishing company.

AUTUMN FAULKNER (MLIS, University of Alabama, 2011) supervises a team of copy catalogers at Michigan State University Libraries, and has experience with special formats, non-English materials, and catalog project management. Current interests include resource description workflows and logistics, future linked data environments, and issues of inclusion, equity, and ethics in metadata.

MATTHEW GALLAGHER (MLIS, Long Island University, 2011) is currently the Collection Management and Metadata Librarian for the University of the Sciences in Philadelphia. He has held various technical services positions related to acquisitions, cataloging, and systems during his career in academic libraries. Previously, Matt worked in the entertainment industry as a business manager and royalty accountant.

NICOLE SMELTEKOP (MILIS, Wayne State University, 2006) is a Special Materials Catalog Librarian at Michigan State University where she catalogs posters, manuscripts, and maps. She also is a member of the digital repository team, where she assists in metadata creation and management. Prior to her transition a catalog librarian in 2014, she was an archivist for eight years.